Betting
on
Blackjack

BETTING ON BLACKJACK

A Non-Counter's Breakthrough Guide
to Making Profits at the Tables

FRITS DUNKI-JACOBS

ADAMS MEDIA
AVON, MASSACHUSETTS

Published by
Adams Media, an F+W Publications Company
57 Littlefield Street, Avon, MA 02322. U.S.A.
www.adamsmedia.com

ISBN: 1-58062-951-2

Printed in Canada.

J I H G F E D C B A

Library of Congress Cataloging-in-Publication Data
Dunki-Jacobs, Frits.
Betting on blackjack / Frits Dunki-Jacobs.
p.   cm.
ISBN 1-58062-951-2
1. Blackjack (Game) 2. Gambling systems. I. Title.
GV1295.B55D86   2003
795.4'23--dc21   2003008273

This publication is designed to provide accurate and authoritative information with
regard to the subject matter covered. It is sold with the understanding that the publisher is not engaged in rendering legal, accounting, or other professional advice. If
legal advice or other expert assistance is required, the services of a competent professional person should be sought.
—From a Declaration of Principles jointly adopted by a Committee of the American
Bar Association and a Committee of Publishers and Associations

Many of the designations used by manufacturers and sellers to distinguish their prod-
ucts are claimed as trademarks. Where those designations appear in this book and
Adams Media was aware of a trademark claim, the designations have been printed with
initial capital letters.

This publication is designed to provide an independent viewpoint and analysis of the
subject matter. The publisher and the author disclaim all legal responsibility for any
personal loss or liability caused by the use of any of the information contained
herein. Questions on how to obtain the software developed for this analysis may be
directed to *Fritsdj@botmail.com.*

This book is available at quantity discounts for bulk purchases.
For information, call 1-800-872-5627.

DEDICATION

A s time has marched on for me over the years, my obsession to finish this work has been tolerated by so many who are close to me in one regard or another. Many thanks go to my sister, Joanna, who gave me a base of operation for my numerous research trips to Nevada in the early nineties; to my nephews, Sean and Zach, for being my strategy testers after many experimental evening sessions; and finally to my parents who always kept me aware of the fact that too much indulgence of anything is usually not appropriate or healthy. And yes, that statement rang so loud and clear with respect to gambling; how those words have always echoed in my mind and protected me when my tendencies to play more than might be responsible would start to get me restless. Thanks also go to my good friends Gary C., Craig, Gene, Matt, and Todd, whose constant support and friendship have carried me through some of the toughest times in my life; without them, this work may have never have been written and completed.

Special thanks go also to Bill Jelen of MrExcel.com, who was always there when I needed that all-important immediate assistance in design modifications to the various analytical betting models that are the basis for much of this book.

CONTENTS

INTRODUCTION

Writing this book is something I felt strongly about for a few reasons. My first intention was to bring all the knowledge I accumulated over the years into one meaningful document—information that I felt needed to be sorted out. My second was to help the average John Q. Citizen understand some issues, not just about the game, itself, but about the psyche—the emotional roller coaster most of us ride when playing this crazy game—and how to control and understand oneself before entering the battle. It's quite frustrating seeing my fellow players get upset, lose their cool, and surrender their money because of a total lack of discipline and self-control, not to mention that in my estimation 99% of the players have no clue about proper playing and betting strategies in any situation, whether it's 21 or any other casino game. The last reason I wanted to write this book is that many of my friends have asked me to get these techniques into a medium they could study, and I figured now is the time.

Much has been written about this game. There are so many books on 21—otherwise known as blackjack—that it's hard to count them all. Most of them deal with understanding how to count cards, which is a legitimate and important topic for blackjack aficionados, but I wanted to do something different. I wanted to show readers what the actual probabilities are in winning this game without getting way too technical, and how to apply those probabilities to a winning strategy. I've read so many books on blackjack that discuss indices, the true count versus the running count, and so on.

I've tried to count cards according to systems developed by the various recognized experts in the field, and all I succeeded in doing was getting a severe headache playing the game due to the amount of concentration and focus I had to put into play at the tables. I do believe that each one of these authors has done important work on the counting topics; however, I firmly believe that counting cards adds only a slight edge to the game over the long run. Furthermore, I believe the methods I employ assist me in deriving greater satisfaction playing the game rather than wrestling with it, not to mention giving me the same amount, if not more, profitability at the end of the day.

It is my sincere hope that after you read this book you may see in yourself the same mistakes I've made and will learn how to correct them as I have. I also want all those who read these pages to know that I really think this game can be beaten—not by the sheer mathematics and probabilities that exist, but with all the *discipline* and *patience* you can muster. These are the two essential ingredients you must have in order to even think about gambling and winning on a regular basis.

A Bit of Philosophy

If you are like me, you're probably fascinated with the idea of making money the easy way, right? Maybe, or maybe not. Well, I'm not ashamed to say that *was* one of my primary motivations for analyzing the game of 21 for the last twenty-five years. My secondary motive was that I wanted to walk into any casino or resort and make a serious run on the tables anytime I wanted and be better at the game than the average Joe Schmoe. I don't know, call it vanity if you like, but there's nothing better or more exciting than cleaning up at the 21 tables! There's nothing like having a group of people hovering around the table, envying your skill, luck, and, of course, your heaping and ever-increasing bankroll. However, getting to that point took a lot of time, money, and anguish. As the old clichés go: "Nothing easy is worth having," and "No pain, no gain!" Yes, you've heard them all. I believe I've suffered enough pain for at least ten men, but, hey, nobody twisted my arm to get into this game either! The bottom line is, if you really want to be good at 21, you've got to suffer a bit—but not too much, because the words written here will potentially take a lot of the pain away. However, nothing replaces preparation, skill, strategy, patience, and discipline—but mostly patience and discipline, which are the *real keys!*

I'm writing these pages to offer the *intermediate* to *serious* player some insight into the game of 21, also known as blackjack, that goes way beyond the beginner's ABCs. *I'm assuming at this point you know the basics of the game and they do not have to be explained.* Offering a different perspective on how to possibly win at this game other than card counting may be refreshing for a change. Most who do use the "count" aren't having a whole lot of fun playing the game; they're just concentrating on the cards coming out and that's it. Not that there's anything wrong with that, it's just that I believe a person can still make money at this game without working so hard at it, and have an element of fun exist without tracking high cards and low cards versus all cards that have been shown. Now then, playing for *fun* and playing for a *living* are two very different things. I ought to know. I've done it for a living, and believe me when I say that it takes nerves of steel, and a lot of patience and nervous tension to make it, along with plenty of frustration and anguish (not to mention a huge bankroll to make your daily score worth the effort). Playing with a "no fear" attitude is *essential* for a *big score* at the tables.

Again, this book is for the intermediate or serious 21 player. If you want to be good and stand a much better-than-average chance at beating the casinos, these pages will help you do it. I can't promise that you'll win every time, but you will win most of the time. My method is based on the analysis of probabilities that exist in the game. And no, this isn't going to be another "how to play using basic strategy" book. God knows there are enough of them out there! However, it does uncover the proper playing strategy based on certain deck configurations. Most people don't know that 21 playing strategy differs from single to multiple deck configurations, and that how you play your cards can sometimes dramatically change when you go from one to the other. Also, the amount you bet on each hand is also based on the probability of winning the sequence of hands. This is the key component strategy uncovered within this book.

Most folks who go to casinos would, of course, love to win! But do they expect to? Usually not. Why? Because they have this warped idea in their heads that losing is a "given," or that having high expectations is not realistic. I'm so tired of hearing this reasoning from people that I could just scream. How many times have you said to yourself, or heard someone say, "Yeah, I'm goin' out to Vegas to make my donation"? Or "We're goin' up there to lose a little dough and have some fun!" I can't believe it! Here are people who slave all year round to make a living, who complain that they're not getting their bonuses or raises, and yet they have no problem at all blowing one-tenth or one-twentieth of their income at the tables, not to mention the slot machines and video poker. (Don't even get me started on those—casinos literally have a license to steal if they have slots and video poker, and nearly all casinos have them!)

Now then, ask yourself, how can anybody expect to win if they don't prepare themselves? Gambling is a serious business! To win, you have to be serious! Don't think for a moment that the casinos will lie down and let you win because of your good looks or any other reason. Casinos are focused on making your personal funds dwindle by the minute. They make their gaming environments so pleasing, so comfortable, that when you do begin losing, you won't mind so much. It's all a grand deception! I'm not saying that when you go on vacation or take a weekend off to go to a gaming resort that you can't have fun; I am emphasizing that when you're at the tables, be serious, be skilled, stay focused, know your game, odds, and limitations—both mental and financial. Most of all, know yourself!

We will analyze the various playing strategies, betting strategies, statistics, and attitudes together, and I hope I will be able to successfully show you that counting cards is not the *only* way to win at this game. Many of the strategies that I will impart here will sound extremely unorthodox to many experienced players and professionals; however, please remember this expression as you are reading: "The proof is in the pudding!" Don't believe me; just watch for yourself. Stand at a table and watch the action. You'll see that the strategies I lay out for you in the upcoming chapters actually do play out. And remember, the most important ingredient is *discipline*— without it, everything I talk about here and in the coming chapters is meaningless!

CAN YOU REALLY WIN PLAYING THIS GAME?

The *real* answer is *no*. You really weren't expecting that, were you? Well, you really can't win—at least not for long stretches at the tables. The house's edge will most certainly grind your stake to zero dollars. Believe me, it's almost a mathematical certainty. The longer you expose your money to the casinos, the greater the chance of your taking it in the shorts. Then why are you reading this book? Because you *can win* in the *short term!* "Short term" by my definition is any realistic profit goal that can be attained in less than two hours. Now, there's a caveat to this statement: You, the player, must be prepared to stay for as long as it takes to reach your profit or loss goal, and that may take longer than two hours! Sometimes you'll get stuck not reaching either, which is known as "trading dollars with the casino," and, if this happens, my advice is to just get up and leave with maybe marginal profits. Take a break and find a table that isn't as static as the one you left. This situation happens to all of us, and it's just a part of the weird phenomenon that happens when playing this game.

The real question here is *do you really want to win?* I ask this question because I am convinced that some people just don't want to! They refuse to correlate being a winner with acquiring the skill it takes to be one. If you had to perform brain surgery and didn't have the training, what would be the chances of performing this surgery successfully? Not very good, I think. But there are literally hundreds of thousands of folks annually trying to perform the equivalent of brain surgery at the tables for which they really have no training, and—here's the funny part—most of them aren't interested in getting it either. It's crazy, isn't it? Folks spend a week studying which new refrigerator or big-screen television to buy but won't spend one second analyzing the games of chance that they often spend two to three times as much time on when they are vacationing or on a gaming outing. I believe it's mainly because they really don't understand the magnitude of how much they really don't know before they begin playing. The lights, marquees, and sounds in the casinos all distract and encourage them to plunk down their hard-earned money and cry "to hell with the odds, full speed ahead!"

It's so funny, when I fly into Las Vegas everyone on the plane is excited and bragging how they will rake in the bucks and clean the unholy Vegas clock; but on the way home I can almost hear a pin drop on the plane. Everyone is always so solemn. Of course, *they're* the ones who just got their clocks cleaned. They weren't defeated by Vegas but by their own lunacy, but will they admit that? I don't think so!

I'd be willing to wager that fewer than 1% of the visitors who come to Las Vegas or any other gambling mecca have taken the time to train themselves for the game of 21, or any other game for that matter. As long as folks believe they can do battle with no weapons or training, those casinos will keep getting bigger and brighter as each year passes. I hope I will be able to drive that point home as we continue—which reminds me of a story with a good ending that illustrates my point exceptionally well.

I was on one of my research trips in the early nineties and met a young man, about the age of twenty-one or twenty-two, playing at the 21 tables in Reno. It turned out this was his last extravagance before shipping out on a submarine. He and I started talking about the game, and he said he didn't know much about it but figured he might make a few bucks before shipping out. I asked him how long he'd been playing at this table and he said just about three hours but wasn't doing real well. He had about $110 in front of him and was betting just $5 on each and every hand. As we talked he continued to lose about $10 every five minutes, and I knew he wasn't going to last very long. I asked him if he'd ever picked up a book on the game, and he said no, but he'd played aboard ship all the time and knew the very basics. He complimented me on my play, realizing that in my playing for just ten to fifteen minutes that I had almost doubled my initial buy-in. He asked how I knew how to play certain hands and how much to bet and would I help him out. Well, normally I won't do that because I hate having the responsibility for someone else's money, which by the way, is always great advice to keep in mind. Being somewhat of a pushover, knowing what it's like being a lonely serviceman ready to ship out, I agreed to help him only if some conditions were met—that he'd first take a time-out and have a drink with me so we could discuss the game a bit, and second, that he would follow my direction at the tables while I explained to him why we were making these moves. He agreed, and off we went to have a drink and talk.

We talked for almost two hours. I even starting writing strategies out on napkins, coasters, you name it. He was totally engrossed in the lessons I was trying to impart, asking all the right questions. I could tell he was absorbing everything—after all, he was a nuclear technician so I knew he had the ability to apply what I was teaching him. We finished with the lessons in the bar and off we went to the another casino to try our luck. On the way there he said he was down about

400 bucks and had only about another $400 left. I told him we'd use the conservative method and take it slow, and he agreed.

We finally wandered into a casino that had an empty $5 table. Everything looked great, and it was even a double-deck game, which was very fortunate as well. We were also fortunate because the dealer was too young to know how to mechanic the cards. In Reno and Tahoe, double deck is dealt from the hand, so if I'm up against a dealer who looks over thirty-five and admits to dealing for ten years or more, with most of that time at the casino where I'm playing, I get really nervous. I've never won in that situation. What are the odds on having a real shot at winning? I'll make book that those odds are really low, meaning it happens rarely, meaning some of the dealers are definitely not on the up and up!

At any rate, back to the story. My new friend bought in for $200 and took my direction on play. I helped for about an hour or so, and he really started kicking it in high gear on his own. By the time a couple of hours had lapsed, he'd won almost $300 back and was making an unbelievable comeback. He applied everything we'd discussed and his confidence lit up the table. I'd given him a playing strategy card for the double-deck game, and he was following those strategies pretty much to the letter and making some adjustments along the way. I went to get something to eat, and he decided to continue to play, which is a smart thing to do—when you're winning, you should never leave the table. When I came back, he'd amassed another $425 in addition to the $300 he'd won before I left. I smiled like a proud father, wished him continued success, and turned in for the evening to get some rest. Before I departed, he thanked me profusely and said he would take some of the money he'd won and buy every book on blackjack that he could get his hands on before shipping out. So there it is—a little training can go a long way if you're inclined to want to understand the dynamics of the game.

CHOOSING THE RIGHT PLAYING ENVIRONMENT

Making the decision on where to play is similar to choosing your favorite place to take a new date or significant other for dinner. You want to make sure that the menu has the right kind of food, great wine, and great service, all of which will optimize your chances of having a terrific night out. Deciding where to play blackjack is no different. Make sure you play at an establishment that provides the key components for you to optimize a winning trip should always be your prime concern.

This chapter offers guidelines on finding a casino with the right deck configurations and the most liberal variations on the rules of play, analyzing the play of others before you sit down at the table, watching the dealer, and, last, watching the floor supervisors (or pit bosses).

Finding the Right Casino

As amazing as this sounds, many supposed veteran blackjack players still don't understand how certain betting options and rule variations can affect their play and chances for continued win opportunities. They still believe that blackjack is blackjack, six, eight, single deck, whatever. Sure they know the game, but do they really understand the rule variations? Most of them don't. At any rate, the casino with the best options for play is where you want to plunk down your money. Lucky for us, these rule variations are becoming increasingly more important in casino marketing. Casinos now realize that blackjack players are smarter about the game and are looking for the most favorable conditions in which to play. This is becoming noticeable in, for example, the downtown Las Vegas casinos, which provide more favorable rules for playing to offset the fact that they are not in the mainstream of Las Vegas tourist flow.

Playing Against the Right Deck Configuration

To maximize your winning opportunities, you should play against the right deck configuration. Given a choice, you should play the following deck configurations, which I've listed from the most preferable to the least preferable. I've also listed for each one the associated *approximate* positive or negative house-edge percentages against (–%) or for (+%) the player.

Single deck (–.2%). Of course this is the most favorable deck configuration because it offers the least probability of extended losing streaks, and the greatest opportunity for the win, which is carefully explained in Chapter 4.

Double deck (–.3%). This configuration offers what I feel is a happy medium for most players, especially those who like to play with no more than one to three players at the table. There is less shuffling than with a single deck but almost the same probability in continued losing or winning streaks.

Six-deck shoe (–.42%). As you probably already surmised, this configuration is more likely to have longer extended losing streaks than the first two. The high and low cards can sometimes be clumped in sections of the shoe and subsequently either bury you or be good to you for extended periods, meaning more than a shuffle or two.

Eight-deck shoe (–.5%). This one is even worse than the six-deck shoe. It's the standard for Atlantic City play, but I really don't recommend playing against this type of configuration unless there's nothing else available.

Other Important Rule Variations

Other rule variants that are important to look at (along with their approximated associated house-edge percentages) are:

Dealer stands on soft 17 (+.15%). This variant means the dealer has an ace and a six because after the initial two cards are dealt, he or she is not allowed to draw any more cards. This configuration has the greatest advantage for players because the dealer now does not have the opportunity to better his or her hand.

Dealer hits on soft 17 (–.2%). This variant is the reciprocal of the previous one. If the dealer draws an ace and a six, the dealer is allowed to improve the hand by drawing another card, thus improving the chances of getting a hand somewhere between 17 and 21. Please note that when this situation occurs, the dealer can improve his or her hand with an ace, two, three, or even a four with a one-card draw and not change any condition of the total. If a ten is drawn, then there is no change to the final hand. Total. It's as if the dealer has multiple opportunities to beat your "pat" hand (a hand between 17 and 21 inclusive), which is always a disadvantage to the players.

Double down on *any* two initially dealt cards (+.2%). This is a big one. This option allows players to place an additional bet equal to that of their original bet and take just one more card. This option is generally used when the player has an initial card total of somewhere between 9 and 11 and is hoping to get a ten-valued card against the dealer's up card of ten or less. Another favorable condition to make this play is when the player has a soft total (a hand containing an ace plus a card valued at two through six) against the dealer's up card of six or less. There are various strategies to optimize this play, which are presented in Chapter 5.

Double down on initial two-card totals of 9 through 11 only (–.1%). This option, for obvious reasons, has less of an advantage for players than the previous double-down option. Players are allowed to double their bets only on initial card totals valued at 9 through 11, which definitely limits their opportunities for getting smaller cards to help their hands. In this case players are definitely looking for a ten, a nine, or even an ace to bring them to a strong 20 or 21 total.

Double down after three or more cards are dealt (+.3%). Okay, I know it's hard to believe, but there are casinos in Las Vegas and other places, that will, for competitive reasons, allow you to double your bet after you have received three or more cards! This is a tremendous advantage over the house! My recommendation is that you locate these casinos and give them *all* your action. You'll usually only find this option, when it's offered, on multideck games.

Surrender (+.065%). This is a great strategic option when used effectively. It allows a player to surrender half of his or her bet upon inspection of the initially dealt cards and not complete the hand. Should a player receive a hand with an initial card total between 15 and 16, and the dealer's up card is a nine, ten, or ace (which are strong up cards), and the player believes taking another card might break the hand, the player can signal the dealer that he or she wishes to surrender. The dealer will then take half the player's bet and push the other half back to the player. Surrender comes in two conditions: early and late. Early surrender allows the player to surrender the hand if the dealer's up card is an ace or a ten-valued card *before* the dealer looks to check for a possible blackjack. This is a huge advantage for players. Late surrender means the player is allowed to surrender the initially dealt cards only *after* the dealer has checked for a blackjack—certainly less advantageous for the player, but still not bad if you drew a stiff hand (a hand whose initial total is between 12 and 16). Again, there are strategies for when to surrender against the ten or the ace, which are indicated in Chapter 5 and its associated charts. The surrender option is offered mostly in multideck configurations (games dealt from the shoe); however, many casinos are now offering this option on double-deck games for competitive marketing reasons.

Splitting pairs up to four times (+.16%). Card splitting is a beneficial option if you receive two like-valued cards, but only if and when the split value plus a ten-valued card has a good chance of beating the dealer's hand. It doesn't always need to be a ten-valued card; sometimes a low-value card will end up placing you in a doubling situation, which is also extremely beneficial. When you're allowed to split cards up to four times—this occurs when receiving like cards in a sequence that allows you to option the opportunity again and again—you can, in many cases, leverage a tremendous advantage against the dealer's hand. Again, this option is mostly prevalent against multideck configurations. For example, suppose the dealer is showing a 7 card and you receive two eight-valued cards as your initial hand. Basic strategy indicates that you should *split* the eights into two hands. After splitting those eights, suppose you immediately receive another eight-valued card—you can now make a third hand! Now you begin drawing cards again and here comes another eight-valued card. Of course, you would split that eight as well, and now you have four hands going or a possible chance of getting four eighteens to possibly beat the dealer's possible seventeen! What started out small now becomes a huge opportunity.

Double down after split (+.13%). Here again, you're trying to leverage and maximize each and every opportunity that you're dealt. You would have split the cards initially if you had believed there was an advantage, and now you get a bonus because the next card that you hit on one of the split cards places you in a likely position to double your bet and your advantage at the same time. A quick example: You're dealt a pair of sevens and the dealer has a six showing (this is usually a breaking hand for the dealer). You split the sevens into two separate hands by motioning the dealer with two split fingers and placing another bet equal to the original bet next to one of the separated sevens. Now, the dealer places a card on the first seven to your right and guess what, you get a three; now your hand totals 10! What now? Well, of course you should double down hoping for a ten card! You place an amount equal to that of the amount on the first seven and motion for one card only. Here comes a nine instead of a ten, your total for the hand on the right is 19 and you definitely stand on the hand. Now, you need to complete the hand with the seven on your left; the dealer now places a two on top of that seven, your total is now 9—what now? You double again! You place another bet equal to the bet on that second seven and motion for one card only. You finally get your ten; your total is now 19 again on the second hand and you stand once again. The dealer flips the bottom card revealing an eight for a total of 14 and must draw another card to this terrible card total. The card comes out, and bang! It's a face card and the dealer breaks or busts her hand. You just realized a great opportunity going from a one-unit potential profit to a four-unit profit! Double after split is great when leveraged properly; again there are charts in Chapter 5 showing when this strategy is best employed.

There are numerous combinations for all these options, and the associated percentages change for the various deck configurations. There are many Web sites that will compute your special inquiry or rule variation for any given set of rules variants; one of the best is *www.wizardofodds.com*. I do encourage everyone to find out the rules and options of a casino, compute them on the Internet, and then decide if it's a place where you'd like to play. Believe me when I tell you that gaming meccas like Las Vegas have hundreds of casinos all with different rule variations. The smart player always figures the best odds *before* walking in. Make sure you do the same!

Analyzing How Others Play Before Joining the Game

As you begin to analyze your play, you should also analyze the play of others. After all, how someone plays definitely affects the outcome after each hand is dealt across the table and subsequently determines whether the dealer will break the hand or not. Of course, many players argue this point, but I recommend that you always watch the table action for at least five minutes prior to sitting down. There's nothing worse than sitting down at a $25 table, betting anywhere from $25 to $100, and having some idiot take two minutes to decide how to play his cards or just indiscriminately hit a pair of cards that should never have been hit or stand on cards that should have been hit! This type of play will most definitely irritate you and break your concentration! I especially hate it when this type of player is playing third base (the last position on the table). He almost always takes the dealer's break card when he shouldn't or doesn't take the dealer's lower pat card when he should. (The pat card is the card that makes a hand—somewhere between 17 and 21 inclusive.) Of course, this is totally disruptive! Also, watch out for other players constantly complaining about the cards they're getting. If they can't take the heat, they shouldn't be playing— period, end of discussion! And of course, these complaints can be a monster irritant and certainly a huge red flag not to take a seat at that table!

On one of my research trips to Caesar's in Lake Tahoe in the early nineties, I was playing a $5 table at third base, betting $10 to $15 units with another guy at first base who was playing $25 to $50 hands. It was about 3:00 A.M., the casino was almost empty, we were both doing great, money-wise and conversationally. It was a perfect scenario, the shoe was being good to us, we were on about a twenty-minute streak of predominantly player hands. Well, I knew it was all too good to be true. Here comes this guy, a total "goof" (as they say in the business), in his early forties wearing one of those pro-football windbreakers, stinking drunk, a real class act! He sits down with about $400 in green ($25) chips. He's dealt his hand, a ten and a two. I'm dealt mine, and then the dealer asks the guy on first base if he wants a hit. The first guy plays his cards, and then this goof begins to yell at the top of his lungs, "Nine of hearts—nine of hearts." I think "Is this guy nuts or something?" If he just gets a nine that would be cool! But a nine of hearts, get a grip, fella! Every hand that he hits, split or double, he invariably yells out what he needs with the suit! This, as you might have guessed, was really getting me agitated, plus he couldn't play worth a lick and was drawing cards with no particular strategy that I could recognize! You guessed it, the shoe immediately went sour on us. This guy was drawing cards until the cows came home, and we began losing—big! This crazy man finally left, and we began winning again, which helps reinforce my theory that a shoe's composition can be affected by how many players are playing against it. That's why I highly suggest that you always observe all the players' play prior to sitting down, which will inevitably save you grief, money, time, and unneeded stress, not to mention not having to put up with morons like the one I just described.

To quote a great character, Gordon Gecko, from the movie *Wall Street,* "A fool and his money are lucky enough to get together in the first place!" So if you ever get stuck in a ridiculous situation as I was, stay a couple of hands, but if you lose five straight, win one, and lose five straight again, get the heck away from that table. Let me say this another way: If you lose more than five hands straight (if you're a novice, with a minimum bankroll), leave, and run—don't walk! Don't wait for 21 doom to squash your confidence or your bankroll. Besides, there's nothing worse than starting at a shoe that immediately starts demolishing your bankroll. We're talkin' about not getting a single winning hand! You sit down at a shoe like that, you really have to leave because, in my experience, when it goes like that, your attitude will affect your playing style, the remainder of the shoe, and certainly the session, in almost all cases.

Watching the Dealers

Assuming you've observed the players, what about the dealers? Well, I've always been a true believer in karma, and if you observe the dealer dealing extremely fast and rushing the players, or hear the dealer being rude to the players, or observe the dealer being a stone face, this is bad karma. In some cases the vibes you get from the dealer can really set the tone at the table and affect your judgment. The other players will invariably be hesitant in playing their cards correctly. You'll begin feeling uncomfortable and, in most cases, will begin wishing you'd never sat down. Trust me—I've been there a bunch of times! On the other hand, having the right karma at the table does make the difference regardless of whether it is coming from the dealers or the players.

Once when I was playing at a tribal casino in Auburn, Washington, I passed by a progressive blackjack game where I saw two elderly Chinese ladies playing alone. I stopped and watched for a few minutes, as I always do before sitting down. They seemed to be having great fun just the two of them; they were speaking Chinese and laughing with the dealer and generally playing their hands correctly with great success. Well, I saw everything going right and decided to sit down and join these ladies. After buying in with a couple of hundred dollars, I gently nodded and smiled to these older ladies, and they smiled back. I placed my first bet. Before the cards came out one of the ladies said to me, "You look like Buddha, we will have much luck with you!" The other lady giggled in agreement while watching me blush a little. I'm a stocky guy with a round face so I guess if that bodily distinction makes me resemble Buddha, so be it! The play began and we were all doing pretty well with the first two deals out of the shoe. The next two deals didn't go as well and the Chinese lady who remarked about me looking like Buddha asked if she could rub my stomach for better luck. Well, I must admit, I've seen just about everything, but this request took the cake! Being a "sporting" guy, I said sure, why not, and so she got up out of her chair, walked over to my seat, rubbed my tummy twice, blurted out something in Chinese to the other lady, they both giggled, and then she sat down. Low and behold her next hand was a natural 21, her friend got a 20, and I drew to a 21. The dealer got an 18, and of course we all won the deal. This play went on and on for the next two hours; every time one of them needed better luck or wanted to double down or split, they'd first come to me, rub my tummy, and play their cards! Don't ask me why, but it worked almost every time. It was so unreal; if I could have bottled the karma that night I would have! There's no explaining the situation—it was just there—all around us.

Watching the Floor Supervisors

Floor supervisors and floor persons can be a distraction. If you're a $25 to $50 a hand bettor, they almost always eye your action, or in some cases come up to you and speak with you trying to take your concentration off the game, especially if they suspect that you're counting cards. This is okay sometimes but gets very tedious with any degree of frequency. If this happens to you, find another area or pit to play in, or even consider leaving for another casino. You never know—being bothersome to above-average players could be casino policy! Most casino floor supervisors are instructed to distract certain bettors especially if their bet spread changes more than four to five units in serious action play. This is typical of the old-guard casino floor men, guys who've been at it since the late fifties or early sixties. This is not to say that there aren't really nice floor supervisors in casinos, because there certainly are, and I've met a few extremely-high caliber individuals who really care about making me comfortable while playing and ensuring that I receive everything I need such as dining comps, drinks, rooms, shows, etc. Some are real service-oriented floor personnel, and it's definitely nice to encounter them. I especially like the ones who actually remember my name from trip to trip, even when the time between trips has been weeks or even months; they are amazing when you think about how many folks they encounter in a shift, let alone in a week or a month or even six months!

The Bottom Line

So now, after you have considered all of this, the bottom line should always be that you find a table where you are comfortable. Maybe you like the way the dealer looks, maybe you like looking at one of the players sitting at the table—who knows what your motivation might be. You must, however, pay attention to what is happening at the table (card-wise) before you sit down. If you ask players how the shoe has been and they say, "Oh brother, we've been getting killed!" then for god's sake, don't sit there! If the dealer is just standing there with no one at his table (but all the tables around him are full), put two and two together here—he probably just annihilated the last batch of players. If you make a motion to sit down and the dealer shakes his head no, you are better off taking his advice and moving along. I prefer control, meaning that I decide on everything. I will usually find a table where I can go head-to-head with the dealer—most often at $25 to $100 tables—and set my own environment for play.

That means I control the situation. If I need to add an extra hand to the game I can and will; when I need to drop a hand, I can and will. Nobody is affecting my game! I don't put up with attitudes, complaints, drunks, excessive talkers, smokers (even though I have one occasionally), disruptive party-goers—you get the idea. I'm in and out with a quick profit and a smile on my face because I took the time to choose the right environment—the environment I wanted to play in!

SINGLE DECK AND DOUBLE DECK VERSUS MULTIPLE DECKS

At this point it's important for you to understand that the probabilities of winning with certain deck configurations are really important. No matter how well skilled you are at playing the game, Lady Luck can turn against you and hold funeral services within minutes after you sit down. You can be doing everything right—drawing, doubling down, splitting, and standing on hands exactly as playing strategy tells you to—and still lose! Hey, sometimes it happens— it happens a lot! The composition of the deck or decks just doesn't want to come your way; it's called "bad card fall." I've been in situations where I did everything perfectly. I had a hard 16, the dealer had a ten showing, I'd take a hit and get a four, the dealer would have a ten in the hole, a tough hit for just a *push!* If I had a hard 18, the dealer would have a 19, and so on. And I'm not talking about one or two hands, either, I'm talking ten to fifteen straight hands! It's pure misery at its best!

That's why analyzing a game before sitting down pays off. Chances are if you take the time to watch the game for a few minutes (especially a shoe game) you'll gain a great deal of important information about the composition of the deck or decks. You'll be able to intelligently decide whether or not the dealer is making the 23% to 32% break average, meaning the dealer should be busting about once every 2.3 to 3.2 hands out of ten hands played. If the players at the table are playing as they should, you'll be able to casually track the amount of ten-value cards (ten, jack, queen, king, ace) coming out in ratio to all the other cards, and see if the dealer's up card continually is a ten value or a two through six value, which is beneficial for the players. Much valuable information can be had for the price of merely a few minutes of good observation, because in a *shoe* game a good or bad situation can last a while.

The Dealer's Break Average

There are 312 cards in the shoe, and the dealer places the cut card one and a half decks from the back, which leaves about 240 cards left in play. With three players at the table plus the dealer, you can figure on an average of ten to twenty cards per deal with hitting, splitting, doubling, and so on, or 240 cards divided by an average of fifteen cards, which equals about twelve deals. The dealer should break at least four to six times during the entire play of the shoe. I can recall playing against a six-deck shoe and the dealer broke only two times during the entire shoe, which is almost unheard of! The dealer's break average went down to approximately 10%, subsequently burying all the players at the table. The shoe was really hot for the house, which is one you want to stay away from. Pay very close attention before sitting down! Don't get caught up in the anxiety of trying to get a bet down before the next deal. You can get skinned, cleaned, and fried in five minutes!

Deck Configurations

Multiple-deck games are the best example of games that you really must observe before you jump in. That's because if the cards aren't falling for the players, the streak could last for a long time, sometimes four to six shuffles (if the same sets of cards are used and there's no rotation). Now, that's a lot of time, especially for six- to eight-deck shoes. On the flip side, if you're watching a game that's favorable to the players, that streak could also last four to six shuffles! This is optimum, and you should jump in. However, after sitting down at what you believe is a favorable shoe and you lose four to five straight hands, get up and walk away. Chances are the shoe is beginning to favor the house and you could spend a great deal of money trying to make it come around for the players again! Believe me, I've done it so many times I can't count them all.

Single-deck and double-deck games are not as subject to streaks as multiple-deck games are. If you have a couple of bad shuffles in a row, that's usually the worst it will get. Similarly, if you have a couple of real good shuffles, that's usually the best it will get. The rest we will say is normal distribution of wins and losses. I highly recommend playing against single- or double-deck configurations, especially double deck! The strategy outlined in Chapter 5 for single and double decks is best suited for play.

You'll find that most of the experienced players (the ones betting at $25 and $100 tables) prefer single- and double-deck games. The usual retort heard from inexperienced players about single and double decks is that there is more shuffling than playing occurring at the table. My only response to this statement is, "Would you rather win with more shuffling or lose with less shuffling?"

Generally speaking, most casinos instruct their dealers to shuffle a single deck every one to two hands and to shuffle a double deck when the "cut card" appears, which is usually about eight hands of play going head-to-head with the dealer. Shuffling not only discourages card counters but is necessary if the table has three to five players, because otherwise they'd run out of cards—right? But please understand that all deck configurations will be looked at and studied: single, double, and multideck.

As a side note, even multideck shoes (four to eight decks) have their good points. The dealer can't manipulate the cards—or let's say, while it's not impossible, it's extremely difficult! I realize that I've just opened a can of worms by making that statement because certainly now you're thinking, why even try if casinos cheat? Well, only *some* casinos cheat, and these are some of the obscure smaller ones. The larger ones don't need to cheat because they get enough gamblers coming to their resorts who are extremely bad players and simply dump their money, so cheating is unnecessary. Besides, cheating is generally frowned upon in the legitimate casino community so it's not very prevalent, but that doesn't stop some of them! As long as there are towns like Las Vegas, Reno, Laughlin, and Atlantic City, where huge amounts of cash are bandied about, it's unrealistic for anyone to believe that all the games are on the up-and-up, because it just isn't so, and I don't care how many gaming agents are out there! Remember, a good rule of thumb is, if there's big money in motion, there's always someone out there looking for an angle on how to get it legitimately or otherwise; sadly more often than not, it's the *otherwise!*

PLAYING STRATEGIES FOR STANDARD 21

ow we've come to the meat and potatoes. In this chapter I'll discuss one-third of the overall equation: the playing strategy! For most of you, this discussion won't be a big news flash. But what I show you are the odds associated with playing certain strategies. I ran the statistics through my own computer programs to verify each strategy played in any given situation and I show you the results. The strategies I analyzed are the cornerstone of playing the game of 21. They change if you're a card counter, but the methods I'm showing you have nothing to do with counting cards, so just stick with 'em and I'll guide you through the maze of possibilities and help you understand when you should change your strategies.

I can't emphasize enough the importance of just knowing and memorizing the strategies I'm about to show you. When you're at the tables it is common courtesy to make your hit, stand, doubling, split, and surrender decisions as quickly as you can. Nobody likes a slowpoke, and it becomes very tedious for the other players if you take forever to make up your mind.

Ever heard of a lynch mob? Well, you'll see one comin' when you take too long to decide on your hands. The good news is that most casinos these days allow players to bring in strategy cards. Just the same, it still takes time to refer to them, so knowing the correct strategy ahead of time is better for all concerned. But take the strategy cards anyway; I do, and I've been playing this game forever! You can make your own by copying the playing strategy charts I give you in this chapter.

Remember to Play in the Most Favorable Situation

At the risk of sounding redundant, you should play in the most favorable situation—the single-deck, then the double-deck, and finally, the multideck (four- through eight-deck) shoes, although you hardly ever see four-deck shoes anymore. You'll find more shoe or multideck games than any others because casinos are trying everything at their disposal to place the odds in their favor, not the players! It is sometimes difficult to locate a nice double-deck game with lenient rules; however, they're out there, so try to seek them out first!

Some casinos using double deck allow doubling on *any* two initial cards instead of the nine though eleven only and allow double after split (DAS) and late surrender, as well. If you can locate a game of this nature, give that casino *all* your action. It's the same as finding a craps table that allows ten times odds (10*x*). I can't stress enough that finding the right game is so important. Finding rules that are as liberal as possible at this game only benefits you; it's tough enough to win as it is, so you may as well find rules that give you the most options and flexibility.

Key Points to Follow
1. Use sound money management to determine your betting strategy.
2. Exercise complete discipline when setting your high/low goal limits.
3. Find the casino with the best rules for optimum win.

4. Choose your table carefully—don't be in a hurry!
5. Try not to play with more than two other players at the table.
6. Never play when you are fatigued or tired.

Learn the Basic Strategy

You absolutely need to know the basic strategy whether you are a card counter or not. It is the mathematical basis, or logic, for the best way to play the cards. You modify that strategy using "gut" instinct if you "feel" a card coming, or if you are a "literal" card counter or "casual" card counter, which will be discussed later on. The following four charts show playing strategies for single-deck, double-deck, and multideck black-jack, and my own modified version for playing any type of deck. Most of this is not new; I've run the information through my own computer systems and have come up with pretty much the same outcomes except for a few deviations. Just see which one works the best for you and study it well.

SINGLE-DECK BLACKJACK

HARD HAND STRATEGY
VALUE OF THE DEALER'S UP CARD

YOUR HAND	2	3	4	5	6	7	8	9	10	Ace
9	DD	DD	DD	DD	DD	H	H	H	H	H
10	DD	DD	DD	DD	DD	DD	DD	DD	H	H
11	DD	DD	DD	DD	DD	DD	DD	DD	DD	DD
12	H	H	S	S	S	H	H	H	H	H
13	S	S	S	S	S	H	H	H	H	H
14	S	S	S	S	S	H	H	H	H	H
15	S	S	S	S	S	H	H	H	H	H
16	S	S	S	S	S	H	H	H	H	H
17	S	S	S	S	S	S	S	S	S	S

SOFT HAND STRATEGY
VALUE OF THE DEALER'S UP CARD

YOUR HAND	2	3	4	5	6	7	8	9	10	Ace
Ace, 2	H	H	DD	DD	DD	H	H	H	H	H
Ace, 3	H	H	DD	DD	DD	H	H	H	H	H
Ace, 4	H	H	DD	DD	DD	H	H	H	H	H
Ace, 5	H	H	DD	DD	DD	H	H	H	H	H
Ace, 6	DD	DD	DD	DD	DD	H	H	H	H	H
Ace, 7	S	DD	DD	DD	DD	S	S	H	H	H
Ace, 8	S	S	S	S	S	S	S	S	S	S
Ace, 9	S	S	S	S	S	S	S	S	S	S

PAIR SPLITTING STRATEGY
VALUE OF THE DEALER'S UP CARD

YOUR HAND	2	3	4	5	6	7	8	9	10	Ace
2 - 2	H	SPLIT	SPLIT	SPLIT	SPLIT	SPLIT	H	H	H	H
3 - 3	H	H	SPLIT	SPLIT	SPLIT	SPLIT	H	H	H	H
4 - 4	H	H	H	DD	DD	H	H	H	H	H
5 - 5	DD	DD	DD	DD	DD	DD	DD	DD	H	H
6 - 6	SPLIT	SPLIT	SPLIT	SPLIT	SPLIT	H	H	H	H	H
7 - 7	SPLIT	SPLIT	SPLIT	SPLIT	SPLIT	SPLIT	H	H	H	H
8 - 8	SPLIT	SPLIT	SPLIT	SPLIT	SPLIT	SPLIT	SPLIT	SPLIT	SPLIT	SPLIT
9 - 9	SPLIT	SPLIT	SPLIT	SPLIT	SPLIT	S	SPLIT	SPLIT	S	S
10 - 10	S	S	S	S	S	S	S	S	S	S
Ace-Ace	SPLIT	SPLIT	SPLIT	SPLIT	SPLIT	SPLIT	SPLIT	SPLIT	SPLIT	SPLIT

LEGEND

HIT — H
STAND — S
DOUBLE DOWN — DD
SPLIT THE PAIR — SPLIT

FIGURE 5-1

DOUBLE-DECK BLACKJACK

HARD HAND STRATEGY
VALUE OF THE DEALER'S UP CARD

YOUR HAND	2	3	4	5	6	7	8	9	10	Ace
9	DD	DD	DD	DD	DD	H	H	H	H	H
10	DD	DD	DD	DD	DD	DD	DD	DD	H	H
11	DD	DD	DD	DD	DD	DD	DD	DD	DD	DD
12	H	H	S	S	S	H	H	H	H	H
13	S	S	S	S	S	H	H	H	H	H
14	S	S	S	S	S	H	H	H	H	H
15	S	S	S	S	S	H	H	H	H	H
16	S	S	S	S	S	H	H	H	H	H
17	S	S	S	S	S	S	S	S	S	S

SOFT HAND STRATEGY
VALUE OF THE DEALER'S UP CARD

YOUR HAND	2	3	4	5	6	7	8	9	10	Ace
Ace, 2	H	H	H	DD	DD	H	H	H	H	H
Ace, 3	H	H	H	DD	DD	H	H	H	H	H
Ace, 4	H	H	DD	DD	DD	H	H	H	H	H
Ace, 5	H	H	DD	DD	DD	H	H	H	H	H
Ace, 6	H	DD	DD	DD	DD	H	H	H	H	H
Ace, 7	S	S	S	S	S	S	S	H	H	S
Ace, 8	S	S	S	S	S	S	S	S	S	S
Ace, 9	S	S	S	S	S	S	S	S	S	S

PAIR SPLITTING STRATEGY
VALUE OF THE DEALER'S UP CARD

YOUR HAND	2	3	4	5	6	7	8	9	10	Ace
2 - 2	H	H	SPLIT	SPLIT	SPLIT	SPLIT	H	H	H	H
3 - 3	H	H	SPLIT	SPLIT	SPLIT	SPLIT	H	H	H	H
4 - 4	H	H	H	H	H	H	H	H	H	H
5 - 5	DD	DD	DD	DD	DD	DD	DD	DD	H	H
6 - 6	H	SPLIT	SPLIT	SPLIT	SPLIT	H	H	H	H	H
7 - 7	SPLIT	SPLIT	SPLIT	SPLIT	SPLIT	SPLIT	H	H	H	H
8 - 8	SPLIT	SPLIT	SPLIT	SPLIT	SPLIT	SPLIT	SPLIT	SPLIT	SPLIT	SPLIT
9 - 9	SPLIT	SPLIT	SPLIT	SPLIT	SPLIT	S	SPLIT	SPLIT	S	S
10 - 10	S	S	S	S	S	S	S	S	S	S
Ace-Ace	SPLIT	SPLIT	SPLIT	SPLIT	SPLIT	SPLIT	SPLIT	SPLIT	SPLIT	SPLIT

LEGEND

HIT	H
STAND	S
DOUBLE DOWN	DD
SPLIT THE PAIR	SPLIT

FIGURE 5-2

MULTIDECK BLACKJACK

HARD HAND STRATEGY
VALUE OF THE DEALER'S UP CARD

YOUR HAND	2	3	4	5	6	7	8	9	10	Ace
9	H	DD	DD	DD	DD	H	H	H	H	H
10	DD	DD	DD	DD	DD	DD	DD	DD	H	H
11	DD	DD	DD	DD	DD	DD	DD	DD	DD	H
12	H	H	S	S	S	H	H	H	H	H
13	S	S	S	S	S	H	H	H	H	H
14	S	S	S	S	S	H	H	H	H	H
15	S	S	S	S	S	H	H	H	H	H
16	S	S	S	S	S	H	H	H	H	H
17	S	S	S	S	S	S	S	S	S	S

SOFT HAND STRATEGY
VALUE OF THE DEALER'S UP CARD

YOUR HAND	2	3	4	5	6	7	8	9	10	Ace
Ace, 2	H	H	H	DD	DD	H	H	H	H	H
Ace, 3	H	H	H	DD	DD	H	H	H	H	H
Ace, 4	H	H	DD	DD	DD	H	H	H	H	H
Ace, 5	H	H	DD	DD	DD	H	H	H	H	H
Ace, 6	H	DD	DD	DD	DD	H	H	H	H	H
Ace, 7	S	DD	DD	DD	DD	S	S	H	H	H
Ace, 8	S	S	S	S	S	S	S	S	S	S
Ace, 9	S	S	S	S	S	S	S	S	S	S

PAIR SPLITTING STRATEGY
VALUE OF THE DEALER'S UP CARD

YOUR HAND	2	3	4	5	6	7	8	9	10	Ace
2 - 2	H	H	SPLIT	SPLIT	SPLIT	SPLIT	H	H	H	H
3 - 3	H	H	SPLIT	SPLIT	SPLIT	SPLIT	H	H	H	H
4 - 4	H	H	H	H	H	H	H	H	H	H
5 - 5	DD	DD	DD	DD	DD	DD	DD	DD	H	H
6 - 6	H	SPLIT	SPLIT	SPLIT	SPLIT	H	H	H	H	H
7 - 7	SPLIT	SPLIT	SPLIT	SPLIT	SPLIT	SPLIT	H	H	H	H
8 - 8	SPLIT	SPLIT	SPLIT	SPLIT	SPLIT	SPLIT	SPLIT	SPLIT	SPLIT	SPLIT
9 - 9	SPLIT	SPLIT	SPLIT	SPLIT	SPLIT	S	SPLIT	SPLIT	S	S
10 - 10	S	S	S	S	S	S	S	S	S	S
Ace-Ace	SPLIT	SPLIT	SPLIT	SPLIT	SPLIT	SPLIT	SPLIT	SPLIT	SPLIT	SPLIT

LEGEND

HIT	H
STAND	S
DOUBLE DOWN	DD
SPLIT THE PAIR	SPLIT

FIGURE 5-3

MODIFIED STRATEGY

ANY DECK PLAYING STRATEGY

HARD HAND STRATEGY
VALUE OF THE DEALER'S UP CARD

YOUR HAND	2	3	4	5	6	7	8	9	10	Ace
9	H	H	DD	DD	DD	H	H	H	H	H
10	H	DD	DD	DD	DD	DD	DD	H	H	H
11	H	DD	DD	DD	DD	DD	DD	DD	H	H
12	H	H/S	H/S	S	S	H	H	H	H	H
13	H/S	H/S	H/S	S	S	H	H	H	H	H
14	H/S	H/S	H/S	S	S	H	H	H	H	H
15	S	S	S	S	S	H	H	H	SR/H	H
16	S	S	S	S	S	H	H	SR/H	SR/H	SR/H
17	S	S	S	S	S	S	S	S	S	S

SOFT HAND STRATEGY
VALUE OF THE DEALER'S UP CARD

YOUR HAND	2	3	4	5	6	7	8	9	10	Ace
Ace, 2	H	H	H	D/H	D/H	H	H	H	H	H
Ace, 3	H	H	D/H	D/H	D/H	H	H	H	H	H
Ace, 4	H	H	D/H	D/H	D/H	H	H	H	H	H
Ace, 5	H	H	D/H	D/H	D/H	H	H	H	H	H
Ace, 6	H	D/H	D/H	D/H	D/H	H/S	H	H	H	H
Ace, 7	S	D/H	D/H	D/H	D/H	S	H/S	H	H	S
Ace, 8	S	S	S	S	S	S	S	S	S	S
Ace, 9	S	S	S	S	S	S	S	S	S	S

PAIR SPLITTING STRATEGY
VALUE OF THE DEALER'S UP CARD

YOUR HAND	2	3	4	5	6	7	8	9	10	Ace
2 - 2	H	SPLIT	SPLIT	SPLIT	SPLIT	SPLIT	H	H	H	H
3 - 3	H	H	SPLIT	SPLIT	SPLIT	SPLIT	H	H	H	H
4 - 4	H	H	H	H	H	H	H	H	H	H
5 - 5	H	DD	DD	DD	DD	DD	DD	H	H	H
6 - 6	SPLIT	SPLIT	SPLIT	SPLIT	SPLIT	H	H	H	H	H
7 - 7	SPLIT	SPLIT	SPLIT	SPLIT	SPLIT	SPLIT	H	H	H	H
8 - 8	SPLIT	SPLIT	SPLIT	SPLIT	SPLIT	SPLIT	SPLIT	H	H	H
9 - 9	SPLIT	SPLIT	SPLIT	SPLIT	SPLIT	S	SPLIT	SPLIT	S	S
10 - 10	S	S	S	S	S	S	S	S	S	S
Ace, Ace	H	SPLIT	SPLIT	SPLIT	SPLIT	SPLIT	SPLIT	H	H	H

LEGEND

HIT	H
STAND	S
DOUBLE DOWN	DD
SPLIT THE PAIR	SPLIT
DOUBLE IF ALLOWED, OTHERWISE HIT	D/H
HIT IF BIG % HIGH CARDS HAVE JUST COME, OTHERWISE STAND	H/S
SURRENDER IF ALLOWED, OTHERWISE HIT	SR/H

FIGURE 5-4

Each of these charts has three sections: hard hand strategy, soft hand strategy, and pair splitting strategy.

Strategy #1: Hard Hand Strategy

The first strategy is the hard hand strategy. We call it that because it refers to the hard total of the first two cards you are dealt, meaning any card total not containing an ace or a pair of cards with the same value. For example, you're dealt a seven and a five; thus your total is a hard 12. If you have a six and an eight, you'd have a hard 14, and so on. It's important to note that you will use the hard hand strategy even if you have more than two cards. For example, if you have a four and a three and you are dealt a two, then another four, you would still draw another card if the dealer had a seven or higher because you have a hard 13. Look at the tables in Figure 5-1 and note the strategy you should take if you're dealt a hard 12 and the dealer has an eight as his up card. Look across the "12" column until you reach the dealer's "8" column and you'll find the recommended strategy. Your strategy in a single-deck game would be to hit.

Strategy #2: Soft Hand Strategy

The second strategy is the soft hand strategy, which is used when one of the initial two cards you're dealt is an ace. For example, if you're dealt an ace and a four, your total is 5 or 15. In a double-deck game (see Figure 5-2), if the dealer had a six as his up card, according to the soft hand strategy section you would double down, meaning you would double your original bet and take only one card. An important note: If, for example, you play the ace and six and are hit with a seven, you now have a hard 14 and should now play the remainder of your hand using the hard hand strategy section. Again, I'm assuming you understand the basics of hitting, standing, doubling down, splitting, and the surrender option.

Strategy #3: Pair Splitting Strategy

The third section of the charts shows the pair splitting strategy, which is used when the initial two cards you are dealt have the same value—two threes, two sevens, and so on. If you were playing at a multideck game (see Figure 5-3), and you were dealt two threes and the dealer was showing a seven card up, according to the pair splitting strategy section you would split the pair. To signal to the dealer that you'd like to split, you would point to, but not touch, your cards, and place a bet amount equal to the original bet near the two cards. After the dealer separates the pair, you would continue to play the first card in the pair according to the hard, soft, or even pair splitting strategy until you've gone as far as you can or have broken the hand. Then you would play the next card of the original split and continue playing as you did the first split card.

Strategy #4: A Conservative but Effective Strategy

As I indicated earlier, I developed three charts for playing single, double, and multideck configurations (Figures 5-1 through 5-3) through computer analysis. This means that if you were to play millions of hands with each strategy, the computer would indicate which strategy is the most profitable. But in reality we don't go to a casino to play millions of hands—we'd either run out of money or die in the process of playing. However, through years of experience and being somewhat conservative, I developed a strategy chart (Figure 5-4) that is good for most any deck configuration but is especially good for single and double deck. My strategy allows you to maximize the hands you are dealt without hanging your butt out of the window. You aren't splitting eights to ten cards; you aren't doubling nine to the dealer's two card, and so on. So in a nutshell, it's conservative yet effective!

Many experienced players take exception with my strategy, but hey, I'm the one who's writing this book, and I've learned that I need to change my playing strategy to stay in the winner's circle, so why shouldn't I share it with you? The reason I even offered Figures 5-1 through 5-3 is because mathematically they are the best plays. But my strategy in Figure 5-4 is one I, and my colleagues, use from time to time as a more conservative guideline.

It's important to note that all these playing strategies are used in concert with your betting strategies, which I discuss later, beginning in Chapter 9. The playing strategy chart may say to split your cards or even double down, but you might be in a betting level that indicates you shouldn't do it. I highly recommend you refer to this chapter as you analyze betting strategies because they do work together.

The playing strategy charts in this chapter have been designed for you to copy and cut out so you can keep them handy at the casinos, and yes, you can use them while at the tables, too. I recommend that once you copy them (reduce them to whatever size fits your needs) and cut them out, you should trim them down and laminate them to protect them against spilled drinks, stains, and even loss. It's hard to lose cards of that size, especially if they're somewhat large and stiff.

PROBABILITIES OF WINNING AND LOSING CONSECUTIVE HANDS

N ow we have to examine what our chances are of winning or losing multiple hands consecutively. To do that, we'll work with a chart I created that clearly depicts the probabilities. The figures on the chart were generated by taking the number two to the sixteenth power (2^{16}) to simulate wins versus losses over thousands of hands of play, not taking into consideration ties, or as they are sometimes called, pushes. The results were rounded and evened up for our basic analysis. If you look at Figure 6-1, you'll see two ways of interpreting the results regardless of the deck configurations.

Consecutive Hands Won by Player	Number of Times	Total Hands	Percent Probability
18	0.5	9	0.00170%
17	1	17	0.00325%
16	2	32	0.00610%
15	4	60	0.01145%
14	8	112	0.02135%
13	16	208	0.03965%
12	32	384	0.07325%
11	64	704	0.13430%
10	128	1280	0.24415%
9	256	2304	0.43945%
8	512	4096	0.78125%
7	1024	7168	1.36720%
6	2048	12288	2.34375%
5	4096	20480	3.90625%
4	8192	32768	6.25000%
3	16384	49152	9.37500%
2	32768	65536	12.50000%
1	65536	65536	12.50000%
Totals		262,134	50.00000%

Consecutive Hands Won by Dealer	Number of Times	Total Hands	Percent Probability
18	0.5	9	0.00170%
17	1	17	0.00325%
16	2	32	0.00610%
15	4	60	0.01145%
14	8	112	0.02135%
13	16	208	0.03965%
12	32	384	0.07325%
11	64	704	0.13430%
10	128	1280	0.24415%
9	256	2304	0.43945%
8	512	4096	0.78125%
7	1024	7168	1.36720%
6	2048	12288	2.34375%
5	4096	20480	3.90625%
4	8192	32768	6.25000%
3	16384	49152	9.37500%
2	32768	65536	12.50000%
1	65536	65536	12.50000%
Totals		262,134	50.00000%

FIGURE 6-1

For example, if you want to know your chances of experiencing a winning sequence of four consecutive hands in a row, find the number four in the left-hand column and the percentage in the far right-hand column, which shows 6.25%. Thus, you have a maximum 6.25% chance of winning four hands in row. Having this information helps you determine that you need to reduce your bet to the table minimum.

This information also helps you if the dealer wins more than three hands in a row. Now the odds are working for you! You now have a 59.375% chance of winning the next hand! Not bad, eh? So how did we reach that number 59.375%? Well, if you don't take pushes into consideration (they occur about 8% to 12% of the time) and split the remainder 50/50 between wins and losses between the player and the house, with a very slight edge going to the house because of the game's edge, the more wins experienced by the house really increases the opportunity for a player to win! If the house wins four hands straight, and you know this occurs 6.25% of the time, you also know that to reach that point the house has already won three hands in a row or 34.375%. You add the additional 6.25% to that amount, making it 40.625%. Then subtract the 40.625% from the 50% chance of the house win occurrences, which gives you a –9.375% chance against another win for the house. Add that amount to the 50% chance that the player will win a hand, and you get a 59.375% opportunity for a player win. It's just that simple!

As you can see, the more straight wins the house gets in a row, the greater the chance the player will win the next hand. Based on this information, you can now construct a base-betting schema that will help you determine what your next bet needs to be based on outcomes.

The preceding chart is the primary basis of analysis and discussion for some of the betting strategies discussed in Chapters 9 and 10. Based on the mathematical probability, you can now begin to understand that no matter what the configuration of the single deck or shoe is, you will win a hand usually within every four to five hands dealt. This is not to say that it's improbable you'll lose, let's say, eight hands in a row, but it is quite unlikely, especially playing against a single-deck or double-deck game. Don't forget that you are trying to reach a profit goal (explained in detail a little later) *before* you hit a long losing streak of hands. The likelihood of reaching that goal is really excellent, so get excited because the good news is coming! It is important to note that these probabilities are also based on playing perfect 21; hitting, doubling, splitting, and standing as required, as indicated in the playing strategy charts in Chapter 5.

ESTABLISHING YOUR STAKE AND SESSION MONEY

One of the biggest mistakes I see folks make is not knowing how much money they need to bring to the tables. It seems as though folks indiscriminately choose tables that don't match their bankrolls. Why? I'll see some poor schmoe reach into his wallet right after payday, pull out 300 bucks, start betting $25 chips, get mad after toasting all that money in about fifteen minutes, and wonder what the heck happened? In this chapter you'll discover why it happened, and how to remedy the situation and similar ones if they happen to you.

Session Money

A session is any period of time during which you sit down and play. It's a predetermined mental commitment to reach a certain profit or loss goal—profit is the goal, of course!—within a certain amount of time. Because you are not always successful winning a session right off the bat, you need to divide your bankroll into segments to assure some sort of longevity for the battle at hand. Think of it this way: Showing up at the tables without the proper bankroll and associated session packets is like showing up on a battlefield with rifles and no bullets! And no one in his right mind would do that, would he?

The Relationship Between Session Money and Stake

Your session money and your stake (bankroll) are directly linked: Session money should always be a minimum of 40 times x, with x equaling your basc betting unit or the table minimum (they could be different). Let's say x equals $5; therefore your session money is $200 (40 x 5). For a minimum of three sessions, your stake or bankroll should equal 3 x $200 or $600 in total. You should have the entire $600 on you *before* walking into the casino. Preferably you should have no ATM or debit cards with you! You should always take a minimum of three sessions' worth of money with you to the casino in the event you lose the first session's stake and you still feel good about playing and want to continue. The following pages list a sampling of some strategies you might use. Remember the minute you win eighteen to twenty units (discussed later) or have played eighty minutes, whichever comes first, then leave the table! Now there's a variation to that we'll be covering later on in this chapter. How did we arrive at the 18/80 rule? It's pretty easy, actually. It's based on a rate of deals in an hour, usually about 120 if it's just you and another player, and an earning rate of about .65 units per hand, multiply by an estimate of 140 hands—voilá, you'll have close to 18 units in approximately 80 minutes on average.

Remember, this advice is for a recreational player not a professional one. A professional plays by different rules; we're sticking with advice that helps the *serious* recreational player. So, at this point, if you are a recreational player who's squeamish about getting bets too high, then you should probably stick to $3 to $5 tables at the highest. Doing that keeps the session safe and comfortable, limits your exposure if you lose a couple of sessions and go home, and ultimately doesn't hurt you too badly. Besides, if you're a once-a-month player and hang out playing with friends, you'd probably spend as much as a two-session loss buying dinner and having drinks in one evening at any average restaurant or bar. I believe on keeping gambling safe and sane for recreational players—like the Fourth of July!

The chart that follows should be used as a guideline because no one can predict how much you will win or lose in any given session. However, after playing literally hundreds, if not thousands, of sessions, I can definitely tell you this table is pretty close once you've mastered the betting strategies contained in Chapters 9 and 10.

SESSION — BANKROLL & THE BET STRETCH				
UNIT AMOUNT	SESSION AMOUNT	SUGGESTED BANKROLL	WIN RATE PER HOUR	EXTREME BET
$3	$120	$270	$40.50	$45
$5	$200	$450	$67.50	$75
$10	$400	$900	$135	$150
$15	$600	$1,350	$202.50	$225
$25	$1,000	$2,250	$337.50	$375
$50	$2,000	$4,500	$675	$750
$75	$3,000	$6,750	$1,012.50	$1,125
$100	$4,000	$9,000	$1,350	$1,500
$250	$10,000	$22,500	$3,375	$3,750
$500	$20,000	$45,000	$6,750	$7,500
$1,000	$40,000	$90,000	$13,500	$15,000

FIGURE 7-1

Making Adjustments to Your Session Money and Stake

There is an alternative to the eighteen-unit goal and eighty-minute average timetable for completion. You must always remember that the longer you stay at the tables, the better the chance of your losing or hitting a long losing streak, which can be humbling. Believe me, I've been there and done that many times over!

So, the alternate method might be as follows: If you're a $5 bettor and want to make, let's say, twenty units per day, then you might consider betting $10 units and looking for a three- to six-unit goal and getting out! This may take ten or twenty minutes using the forthcoming strategies, but it has its benefits. Although you get out of the game quicker with a smaller gain, you can go to another table or another casino and do it again, making another three- to six-unit hit real fast. Do this three to four times daily and you'll easily make your twenty-unit daily goal; in most cases you'll see an average twenty- to thirty-five-unit gain spread for an average play time of just under two hours. What does that add up to for the hourly win rate? About $75 an hour! That's not bad, is it?

So now you're asking, "What does this have to do with the session and bankroll topics?" The answer is *plenty!* If you adjust for shorter playing time and bigger units, you still have to adjust your total bankroll and session packet sizes. To accomplish the $10 unit size and smaller win goals in a shorter time frame, I recommend a minimum bankroll of $1,000 with session packets of around $330 to $350. I would never recommend trying this escalated and accelerated method with fewer than $40(x)$ session packets with always (3) packets on you because you could get caught in a short-term losing streak and the escalating bets could really get big in a hurry and wipe you out! Again, the important thing is that you have a complementary bankroll that matches your bet units so you can stay in the game.

Here's a story to illustrate this point: bigger units with *no* bet spread. Not too long ago, my buddy and I were just having a drink, sitting on the sidelines (one of the empty, not-in-action blackjack tables) at the local casino, and we saw this guy, lets call him "Marblehead," betting his behind off playing the table maximum, which was $100. By some act of God, he was winning at least 70% to 80% of his bets and making serious money. My friend and I got up and stood by him at the tables and continued to watch for another ten minutes. Marblehead finally invited us to sit down with him and so we did. Each of us pulled out our $200 packets of session money and began to play at the table minimum, which was $5. I was at first base, my buddy in the middle of the table, and Marblehead was holding up at third base.

During our play, we starting conversing with Marblehead and asked him what his buy-in (initial bankroll) was. He said, while pointing to his current stake, that his buy-in was $180 and he'd been playing only about forty-five minutes or so (here again, not enough bankroll and his betting-unit size was too high and not even close to matching it). My buddy and I looked at each other in total amazement because Marblehead had at least $1,200 in black ($100 chips) and another $400 in green ($25 chips) in front of him, not to mention that every five to ten minutes or so he would grab the bundle of currency in his pocket and count up what he had, which was aggravating me to no end because the amount in his pocket never changed! It wasn't as though he was going to the cashier's cage and changing his black or green chips every five minutes. The stake in front of him would vary like an elevator going up and down; one minute he'd be up a couple of thousand, and the next minute he'd be down a thousand. I wanted to handcuff this guy and tell him that he needed to begin betting a spread, starting with $15 to $25 and escalate from there, using my methods. But he would not have any of that; he knew better!

In actuality, he did know better for the short term. By the time he was done (about an hour and half after we'd initially sat down), he amassed about $4,600 betting like a crazy man. He had totally demolished the laws of probability and emerged victorious! But did he? He was totally immersed in victory and felt really good, and my buddy and I were exceptionally happy for him, because we both knew his victory was the ultimate fluke.

So after cashing out, he stood with us for a few minutes to "shoot the breeze" and then it happened—what always happens—he succumbed to greed and the calling of the tables. There was no one sitting at the Spanish 21 table, so sit down he did! He plopped down $1,000 for black chips and started playing. He vaporized that amount in about seven minutes. Out came another $1,000 as he shook his head and said, "I guess I'll get 'em this time!" Wrong. He proceeded to toast another $1,000 in about ten minutes. *No bet spread, not enough session money, not enough bankroll, and definitely not a high enough table limit.* He beat the odds earlier, but now it was time for the odds to catch up to him. As you have probably guessed, old Marblehead got cleaned, skinned, and fried by the time an additional twenty minutes passed; all of what he'd won he lost to the casino, plus his original buy-in money!

This story is, of course, a great example of no discipline; however, the main impact of this illustration is this: If he had just used even a bet spread, he would have won almost twice as much as he did in the first session because every time he lost, he'd lose $100 instead of regressing to a base bet where he would have lost only $25. He was losing $75 more than he had to each and every time he lost. The biggest issue is this: Trying to bet at the table maximum, with no ability to escalate or get a bet spread, eliminates the possibilities of any type of recovery after a series of devastating losses.

Profit Goals and Knowing When to Leave the Table

How much is enough is a question everyone wants answered, don't they? Gambling can be addictive. Most folks have a hard time pulling themselves away from the tables, and that was true for me, too! Knowing when to get up and leave or take a break is a very critical component of playing the game. People rationalize staying on by thinking or saying, "It's not enough profit for the time I spent. I can make a few more bucks and then go." Or "I know things are going to turn around here pretty soon. I'll just stick it out a little more until it does." Yes, you've heard, said, or thought all these things if you've ever been gambling. A key component of success in 21 is knowing not just the playing strategy, but knowing yourself. I finally realized after years of play that the only way to get out with my skin intact and make a tidy profit is knowing how much is enough and to stick with it. Now, I'm happy to say, I've finally turned a corner with a formula that works for me, and I'm including it here for you to try out. The central goal is to win eighteen to twenty units of whatever you are betting.

Step 1: Divide Your Stake into Three Equal Packets

Begin with your session-one money and keep the other two session packets in reserve. The following examples illustrate the options you have in planning your stake using the figures in the Session—Bankroll and the Bet Stretch chart (Figure 7-1):

- If you are playing $3 tables, you need to buy in for $120 in chips (your session-one packet), which is 40 times $3. For three sessions, your total stake is $360 ($120 *x* 3). You need to have this amount on you.
- If you are playing $5 tables, you need to buy in for $200 in chips (your session-one packet) for a total stake of $600 for three sessions. You need to have this amount on you.
- If you are playing $10 tables, you need to buy in for $400 in chips (your session-one packet) for a total stake of $1,200 for three sessions. You need to have this amount on you.

Step 2: Set Your Win and Loss Goal

Once you've bought in to the table, your goal is to make merely 35% to 50% of your buy-in amount on the upside, and 80% of your buy-in on the downside. Here are some examples for different types of tables:

- **$3 table, $120 per session, $360 stake**
  Upside: Leave when your total in front of you is fifty-eight units or $174. Go to Step 3.
  Downside: Leave when the total in front of you has dwindled to $22, and session-one money is now gone. Go to Step 3.

- **$5 table, $200 per session, $600 stake**
  Upside: Leave when your total in front of you is fifty-eight units or $290. Go to Step 3.
  Downside: Leave when the total in front of you has dwindled to $36, and session-one money is now gone. Go to Step 3.
- **$10 table, $400 per session, $1,200 stake**
  Upside: Leave when your total in front of you is fifty-eight units or $580. Go to Step 3.
  Downside: Leave when the total in front of you has dwindled to $72, and session-one money is now gone. Go to Step 3.
- **$15 table, $600 per session, $1,800 stake**
  Upside: Leave when your total in front of you is fifty-eight units or $870. Go to Step 3.
  Downside: Leave when the total in front of you has dwindled to $108, and session-one money is now gone. Go to Step 3.
- **$25 table, $1,000 per session, $3,000 stake**
  Upside: Leave when your total in front of you is fifty-eight units or $1,450. Go to Step 3.
  Downside: Leave when the total in front of you has dwindled to $180, and session-one money is now gone. Go to Step 3.

Step 3: Decide to Stay in or Leave the Game

If you're on the upside and you've met your eighteen-unit profit goal, it's time to take a break and get away from the table. Once you're away from the table, you need to decide if you're still fresh enough to play. Are you still feeling positive and raring to go? If the answer is yes, go back to the table using the same rules and same discipline. If the answer is no, take the money and feel good about the discipline you just exerted. You should feel great once you get home because you just defeated the bad guys and have the dough to prove it.

If you're on the downside and have lost your session-one money but are still feeling positive, fresh, and full of spirit, go to session-two money. Do not confuse wanting to get even with feeling positive—they are not the same. If you are totally negative and mad for losing session-one money, guess what? Time to leave the casino until your head is on straight. Go home. Tomorrow is another day. Let me repeat that. *Go home. Tomorrow is another day!* If you lose session-two money and you're still fresh and feeling positive, go for it; however, I really discourage doing that if at all possible. Session-three money should be used as a last resort only! If you've lost the two previous session money packets, something else is wrong; maybe your attitude is affecting the game, or your judgment in betting and playing is not what it should be. Having thoughts like "I've got to get back to even, can't leave here with them keeping my money!" or "If those other idiot players would just leave I could get the mojo on this table working again and get back to even real quick!" Think about it. If you are using the strategy according to what I've laid out for both playing and betting, it's a black-and-white conclusion. You should have a winning session between the first two packets of session money. If you don't, that should tell you something else is wrong. Could it possibly be you? State of mind is everything in this game. Be careful not to psych yourself out, because it's easy to do.

Is It All That Important to Follow These Steps?

Do you really need to stick with my advice even if you're just a recreational player? The answer is an emphatic yes, *especially* if you are a recreational player! The one thing casinos count on is that you won't show up with enough cash to do battle with them, and in most cases they are correct, aren't they? Ask yourself when was the last time you showed up at a casino using the bankroll amounts I recommend? Or when you showed up, did you go to the ATM and withdraw $40(x)$ of what you needed? Probably never, or at least no more than once or twice before, and that was totally by accident. Again, if you wish to do battle, you have to have enough ammunition to put up the fight!

One more issue: If you've been playing well and are getting eyeballed by the casino managers (pit bosses) due to the variance of your bet (and they will vary!), just pick up your profits and leave. Getting harassed by them is an inconvenience you shouldn't have to put up with. It's just that easy. If you made only $75, so what—you're ahead, feeling good. Move on to another table or even another casino. Do that three to four times a night and you'll be up $300 to $400 in an evening (playing a $3 unit), and that ain't bad! You know the expression "a bird in the hand . . ."? Too many folks try to grind out the big win in one session at the first table where they sit down. This is where the casinos have you by the short hairs because sooner or later those cards turn bad and there you are, trying to get back the profits you'd made earlier plus the session money you started with. Does this sound familiar? Does it sound like you may have done that once or twice? How many times have you said to yourself, "If I'd only quit when I was so far ahead!"? Don't feel bad—we've all been there; it's a common mistake. With the betting strategies I discuss in Chapters 9 and 10, along with the playing strategies in Chapter 5, trying to grind out the big win will be a thing of the past!

THE CURRENT LOSS
BALANCE BETTING STRATEGY—
PROFITS WHILE WINNING OR LOSING

T he really dicey part about playing this game is knowing how much to bet in any given situation.
Understanding what's happening with the cards coming out, understanding the consecutive loss sequence probabilities, and keeping your eye on your session money all play
important factors in staying a winner. Then you need to apply
some of the knowledge gained about the probabilities of winning and losing consecutive hands (Chapter 6) and develop
some feasible betting strategies around that. In this chapter I
explain how to use my current loss balance (CLB) betting
method to keep you safe, even in losing situations. But first,
I want to preface that with a little background theory.

Negative Progression

Let's spend some time talking about negative progression.
Generally, it is frowned upon by most of the professional
gambling community because of its potential for R.O.R. (risk

of ruin), and justly so. The primary method that it is compared to is the Martingale system that tells you to double-up each time you lose, because when you eventually win the loss sequence, you'll win all your money back plus your original bet. *Hmmm,* now let's see what happens if we lose, say, ten times in a row starting at, let's say, $5. Look at the following figure and see where you stand on the Martingale side compared to the CLB side.

MARTINGALE		THE CLB	
"The Old Double-Up"		"Semi-Aggressive Recovery"	
1	($5)	1	($5)
2	($10)	2	($10)
3	($20)	3	($22)
4	($40)	4	($46)
5	($80)	5	($5)
6	($160)	6	($5)
7	($320)	7	($5)
8	($640)	8	($5)
9	($1,280)	9	($5)
10	($2,560)	10	$5

TOTAL	($5,115)	TOTAL	($103)
BET 10 DOUBLED	$5,120	CLB @ 60%	$63
TOTAL WAGERED	$10,235	TOTAL WAGERED	$166
GAIN FROM BET	$5,120	GAIN FROM BET	$63
NET AFTER WIN	$5	NET AFTER WIN	($40)
RISK VS. NET	2047:1	RISK VS. NET	126:1

FIGURE 9-1

So what do we have here? Ten losses in a row (which will happen at some point or another) with the Martingale system means you have spent at least $5,115 from a starting $5 bet and still haven't won yet. Here's the kicker. Let's assume you win bet number eleven of $5,120 (which is the $2,560 doubled) and recover all your losses. By doing so, you have wagered the sum total of $10,235 to win $5! Now, would anyone in his or her right mind do that? I don't think so. Trust me when I tell you that your knees will be doing some serious knocking starting at around the seventh or eighth loss and beyond! The risk versus reward ratio on that is about 2,047:1

versus using my CLB method, which yields a ratio of 126:1. Let me tell you how my method works.

The CLB Method

My CLB betting schema incorporates the probability of successive winning and losing sequences along with a sensible "loss recovery" strategy that will enable a player to suffer ten, fifteen, or even twenty or more losses in a row while keeping the betting safe and sane and recovery inevitable within a reasonable time frame. Does that sound too good to be true? Well, lucky for you, it's not! The problem with negative progression schemes, like the Martingale system, is that the bets get so high they wipe out your session money and possibly even your bankroll in a matter of minutes with no potential for recovery, especially when you experience extended groups of successive losses. I'm happy to report that trying to solve this issue has been in the forefront of my analysis for many years, and now, I'm comfortable in sharing this concept. It's a tiered betting strategy with a main ingredient I call current loss balance (CLB) recovery when losses exceed four to five in a row in the "zone." The zone is the area where we can expect over 81.25% of the win and loss sequences to occur. The remainder of the 18.75% is taken care of by extended wins in the win column and in the loss columns.

The objective is to build a strategy that allows you to do the following:

- Systematically step up and regress (lower) your bets while winning.
- Step up your bets while losing in a very limited way.
- Look for a recovery win that incorporates a profit for your investment.
- Limit the possible loss sequence up to four or five losses in a row (you decide).

- Step all the way down to the base unit until a win occurs (this then becomes the trigger bet).

You then take a percentage of the CLB, let's say 40%, and make that your next bet. If a win occurs on the next bet, you recover 40% of all the losses to that point. Recovering the balance should take only a matter of four to twenty hands on average, depending on the deck configuration and the betting schema that you decide to utilize. If the balance of the action play stays within the zone. Even if the action doesn't stay within the zone, you'll still recover; it will just take a few more hands to get back to where you started before the loss sequence occurred. If you lose your first CLB bet, then betting resumes at the base unit until a win again occurs. Then you begin the second CLB sequence, which covers your initial losses and your first CLB loss. Either way, you will eventually get two wins in a row (enabling the recovery) in winning the CLB bet, and be on the road to recovery and back in the action on the plus side!

Figure 9-2 illustrates a possible scenario going to the fourth losing bet in the zone (counting the one loss from the win column and three in the loss column), then reducing to the base unit in the CLB stage 2, and then making your initial CLB bet. This is one of many scenarios you'll encounter and you'll discover different methods beyond the next example. What's important is that we begin examining the strategy and discussing the various parameters that might be changed using a sample result model of 160 hands played (see Figure 9-5) that we'll be using as a standard for comparative cross-reference against the other strategies that will be discussed.

CLB STRATEGY - MODEL 1
Semi-Aggressive CLB-ZONE Stage Betting
(For a $5 Minimum Table and/or Base Unit size)

Tier Level Betting WIN Schema

Bet Code	Bet Amount	Double or Split OK	Chance of a Player Win	IF WIN GO TO	IF LOSS GO TO
THE ZONE					
W1	$5	Yes	12.500%	W2	L2
W2	$5	Yes	12.500%	W3	L2
W3	$8	Yes	9.375%	W4	L2
W4	$5	Yes	6.250%	W3	L2
CLB STAGE 2					
W5	40-CLB	No	12.500%	W1	L6
W6	40-CLB	No	12.500%	W8	L7
W7	40-CLB	No	12.500%	W8	L7
CLB STAGE 3 - OPTIONAL					
W8	$10	Yes	12.500%	W9	L2
W9	$8	Yes	12.500%	W10	L2
W10	$5	Yes	9.375%	W1	L1

Tier Level Betting LOSS Schema

Bet Code	Bet Amount	Double or Split OK	Chance of a Dealer Win	WHEN WIN GO TO	IF LOSS GO TO
THE ZONE					
L1	$5	Yes	12.500%	W1	L2
L2	$10	Yes	12.500%	W1	L3
L3	$22	No	9.375%	W1	L4
L4	$46	No	6.250%	W1	L5
CLB STAGE 2					
L5	$5	Yes	Variable	W5	L5
L6	$5	Yes	Variable	W6	L6
L7	$5	Yes	Variable	W7	L7

FIGURE 9-2

As illustrated in Figure 9-2, the coded bets W1 and L1 are the initial bets. Follow along with Figure 9-2 as I describe how the betting goes. For example, if you place an initial bet W1 and win, then your next bet would be bet W2. If you win that, then your next bet would be W3, and so on. If you reach bet W4 and win, then your next bet would go back to W3. If that wins, you advance to bet W4, and keep going back and forth until you experience a loss. If at any point in the win sequence you experience a loss, your next bet would be bet L2. In this case, let's say you lose bet W4 at $8, then bet L2 $10 and win, you would recover the $8 loss on bet W4 and profit $2.

Now, let's say you lose L2, you proceed to bet L3 $22, and you win. You would recover the W4 $8 loss plus the L2 $10 loss and profit $4. If you get to the L4 bet and win, you would again recover all subsequent losses, and profit $6.

If you lose on the (L4) bet, you now exit the zone and go into CLB stage 2, a "protection mode," betting only your base unit and limiting your possibilities of continued downside losses. The goal here is to be able to suffer numerous losses from this point on—three, four, six, or possibly more—and still be able to recover in a reasonable amount of time. Once L4 has lost, you bet the base unit until you experience a win; continued losses are no problem because you're losing only the minimum bet.

Once a win occurs (this is your trigger bet), you immediately go into CLB mode; you assess how much you have lost and take a percentage of that loss to determine your next bet amount. Therefore, let's assume for this example you lost the W4 bet of $8, which sends you to the loss column and the L2 bet of $10, which you also lose. Then you lose L3 of $22, and then L4 of $46 for a grand total of $86 in five losing bets. Yes, this betting scenario is pretty aggressive, but you needn't worry because you'll learn many more strategies coming up that may suit you, or you will understand how to construct a strategy that best suits your bankroll, gaming acumen, and nervous tension threshold.

Let's move on to bet L5 and bet only $5. Let's say for this example you lost another two bets of $5 and then experienced a win of $5. The win of $5 cancels one of the two $5 losses so you are now out a total of $91, and that win sends you to bet W5. Again, the win is your trigger bet, and let's say you predetermined that you'd be recovering at a rate of 40%; therefore 40% of the $91 is about $36 (or 40-CLB). If you win this bet, and the probability table says you most likely will, you are only in a –$55 situation making the possibilities for full recovery just a small series of bets away. Upon winning you immediately go to bet W2 and start the sequence all over again. However, let's say you lost your initial recovery bet of $36, now what? You go back to bet L6 and keep betting $5 until you experience a win that again sends you over to the win column and bet W6 for another 40-CLB bet (the 40 meaning the percentage of CLB). You now try the process again hoping for a two-in-a-row win.

It's important to note that the deficiency of not fully recovering the loss in any given series is picked up by the successive wins you experience in the win column (W1 through W4) in addition to repeated recoveries while profiting in the loss column (L1 through L4) and in making your double downs and splits, not to mention the many 21s or blackjacks along the way while working on your L2 through L4 bets. At any point when you win while making the W5 bet, thus recovering (winning), you immediately go to the W2 bet and begin the sequence all over again as indicated in Figure 9-2.

Please take note that if you progress to W6 or W7 CLB bets and win, you can proceed to W8 instead of the W2 bet and begin a *new* stage of escalated betting. *This variation is totally at your option.* The betting schema formalized in Figure 9-2 also indicates the percentages of either the player or the dealer getting these win or loss sequences successively and also articulates whether doubling or splitting is or is not recommended at certain betting levels. This is key to consistent winning. You certainly do not need to expose yourself to an even bigger loss by doubling an L4 or even a 40-CLB bet when it's not required.

It's also important to note that while this variation may seem expensive to use even at a $5 betting level, it works even if you don't use exactly the same schema as long as you build a recovery component into it! The strategy in Figure 9-2 is typically something you might use when you are winning in the short term, three out of five bets. In Figure 9-3, I present a more conservative model for those of you who get a little squeamish going to an L4 bet. And even if that one appears too aggressive, I have even more examples and variations coming up.

In the Figure 9-3 model, we again go only to the L4 losing bet before we revert to the $5 CLB stage 2 protection bets where we begin the CLB sequence. The variables in this schema are flexible; you can change all the parameters to suit your betting comfort levels. I suggest that you don't exceed the 40% CLB factor; the bets will begin to enter the "not so comfortable" zone because they tend to get pretty high after the second CLB attempt. You'll actually find that you can use 30% (30 CLB) as a recovering factor and it will almost pace the 40% time frame for total and complete loss recovery, and that's not bad!

In the next figure, we go to the L4 losing bet before we exit into the CLB arena. This method also works and is designed to keep the bets from getting too crazy and making you uncomfortable. Remember, you are playing because you want it to be fun, not grueling and fraught with tension.

CLB STRATEGY - MODEL 2
Conservative CLB-ZONE Stage Betting
(For a $5 Minimum Table and/or Base Unit size)

Tier Level Betting WIN Schema

Bet Code	Bet Amount	Double or Split OK	Chance of a Player Win	IF WIN GO TO	IF LOSS GO TO
THE ZONE					
W1	$5	Yes	12.500%	W2	L2
W2	$5	Yes	12.500%	W3	L2
W3	$8	Yes	9.375%	W4	L2
W4	$5	Yes	6.250%	W3	L2
CLB STAGE 2					
W5	40-CLB	No	12.500%	W1	L6
W6	40-CLB	No	12.500%	W8	L7
W7	40-CLB	No	12.500%	W8	L7
CLB STAGE 3 -OPTIONAL					
W8	$10	Yes	12.500%	W9	L2
W9	$8	Yes	12.500%	W10	L2
W10	$5	Yes	9.375%	W1	L1

Tier Level Betting LOSS Schema

Bet Code	Bet Amount	Double or Split OK	Chance of a Dealer Win	WHEN WIN GO TO	IF LOSS GO TO
THE ZONE					
L1	$5	Yes	12.500%	W1	L2
L2	$10	Yes	12.500%	W1	L3
L3	$15	No	9.375%	W1	L4
L4	$25	No	6.250%	W1	L5
CLB STAGE 2					
L5	$5	Yes	Variable	W5	L5
L6	$5	Yes	Variable	W6	L6
L7	$5	Yes	Variable	W7	L7

FIGURE 9-3

58

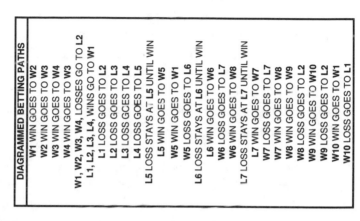

DIAGRAMMED BETTING PATHS
W1 WIN GOES TO W2
W2 WIN GOES TO W3
W3 WIN GOES TO W4
W4 WIN GOES TO W3
W1, W2, W3, W4, LOSSES GO TO L2
L1, L2, L3, L4, WINS GO TO W1
L1 LOSS GOES TO L2
L2 LOSS GOES TO L3
L3 LOSS GOES TO L4
L4 LOSS GOES TO L5
L5 LOSS STAYS AT L5 UNTIL WIN
L5 WIN GOES TO W5
W5 WIN GOES TO W1
W5 LOSS GOES TO L6
L6 LOSS STAYS AT L6 UNTIL WIN
L6 WIN GOES TO W6
W6 LOSS GOES TO L7
W6 WIN GOES TO W8
L7 LOSS STAYS AT L7 UNTIL WIN
L7 WIN GOES TO W7
W7 LOSS GOES TO L7
W7 WIN GOES TO W8
W8 WIN GOES TO W9
W9 WIN GOES TO W10
W9 LOSS GOES TO L2
W10 WIN GOES TO W1
W10 LOSS GOES TO L1

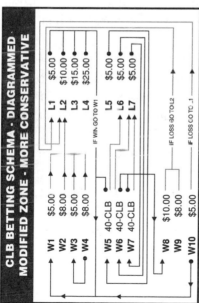

CLB BETTING SCHEMA - DIAGRAMMED
MODIFIED ZONE - MORE CONSERVATIVE

W1	$5.00	L1	$5.00
W2	$8.00	L2	$10.00
W3	$5.00	L3	$15.00
W4	$8.00	L4	$25.00
		IF WIN GO TO W1	
W5	40-CLB	L5	$5.00
W6	40-CLB	L6	$5.00
W7	40-CLB	L7	$5.00
		IF LOSS GO TO L2	
W8	$10.00		IF LOSS GO TO L1
W9	$8.00		
W10	$5.00		

FIGURE 9-4

Sixty to Eighty Minutes of Play

In this section I'll take you through various win/loss scenarios and explain what you can actually do in about sixty to eighty minutes of play. We will be using win/loss results as the comparative model for the strategies that we'll be presenting, just so we can compare apples to apples and analyze the differences. It is also important to note that we did not stop increasing the bet after the fourth loss; we just kept betting according to the progression until we won, just to prove that it's difficult to go beyond five to six losses in a row. The idea behind this philosophy of betting more than two times the losing bet in the early levels is that once you do win, you'll actually win more than the original bet once all is recouped, thus showing a return on your investment. With these types of bets, the more you lose, the greater the profits you realize once the win does come. Remember that more than 81% of the time the action will stay between bets W1 through W4 and bets L1 through L4—this is the *zone!*

As indicated, I do *not* recommend doubling or splitting hands past the third losing bet for obvious reasons. The idea here is to recoup your losses and make a marginal profit upon winning each loss sequence, not walk a high wire! For those of you who wish to go beyond those parameters, you're taking an above-average risk that is *not* required. See the following figures for what sixty to eighty minutes of play really looks like!

Another important note to remember is this strategy can only be employed at higher-limit tables; if playing $10 units, you need a $500 table maximum; for $15 units, you need preferably a $1,000 table maximum, and so on.

As you will see, for about sixty to eighty minutes of play, you can show a decent return on investment (R.O.I.) for all wagers made. This is an important factor to track because you certainly want to make your money grow in relation to the amount of risk and work exerted to make it. Remember, you will do better going head-to-head against the dealer playing one or two hands at the most. You will receive a better distribution of the cards and have fewer issues with folks who are getting the better cards when you're not. The following figures depict what's really happening in the midst of the action. As gamblers and 21 players, we get so caught up in making the bets as we're playing that we don't really stop to analyze who has won more bets—ourselves or the dealers? You should stop and consider how much money is really traveling back and forth between you and the casino or the house (dollars wagered per hour). It's also important to note that in this model of play there are significantly more losing hands than winning ones to the tune of 13% more, which is uncharacteristic of what we would typify as a normal distribution of wins and losses—and yet we still carved out a nice and tidy profit for the session. A reminder, all CLB bets have been rounded to the closest $5 increment for all betting schemas presented in this chapter.

The following figure is extrapolated for 160 hands or about eighty minutes, one to two hands against the dealer. It was calculated for 40% CLB for random results at a minimum $5 to a maximum $100 table limit using Figure 9-2. Our goal, of course, is to make eighteen to twenty units of $5 before hand number 160. Watch the CLB column and see that it accumulates the loss balance as betting proceeds. Let's see what happens in Figures 9-5 and 9-6.

FIGURE 9-5

RANDOM RUN FOR (160) RESULTS — $5 BET UNITS — MODEL 1

HAND NO.	BET CODE	BET AMT	RESULT	GAIN/ LOSS	RUNNING BALANCE	CLB ACCRUAL
INITIAL	W1	$5	PUSH	$0	$0	$0
2	W1	$5	L	($5)	($5)	($5)
3	L2	$10	L	($10)	($15)	($15)
4	L3	$22	WIN	$22	$7	$0
5	W1	$5	WIN	$5	$12	$0
6	W2	$5	WIN	$5	$17	$0
7	W3	$8	L	($8)	$9	($8)
8	L2	$10	L	($10)	($1)	($18)
9	L3	$22	PUSH	$0	($1)	($18)
10	L3	$22	L	($22)	($23)	($40)
11	L4	$46	PUSH	$0	($23)	($40)
12	L4	$46	WIN	$46	$23	$0
13	W1	$5	WIN	$5	$28	$0
14	W2	$5	L	($5)	$23	($5)
15	L2	$10	L	($10)	$13	($15)
16	L3	$22	WIN	$22	$35	$0
17	W1	$5	WIN	$5	$40	$0
18	W2	$5	L	($5)	$35	($5)
19	L2	$10	WIN	$10	$45	$0
20	W1	$5	L	($5)	$40	($5)
21	L2	$10	WIN	$10	$50	$0
22	W1	$5	WIN	$5	$55	$0
23	W2	$5	L	($5)	$50	($5)
24	L2	$10	WIN	$10	$60	$0
25	W1	$5	L	($5)	$55	($5)
26	L2	$10	WIN	$10	$65	$0
27	W1	$5	WIN	$5	$70	$0
28	W2	$5	WIN	$5	$75	$0
29	W3	$8	L	($8)	$67	($8)
30	L2	$10	WIN	$10	$77	$0
31	W1	$5	L	($5)	$72	($5)
32	L2	$10	PUSH	$0	$72	($5)

HAND NO.	BET CODE	BET AMT	RESULT	GAIN/ LOSS	RUNNING BALANCE	CLB ACCRUAL
33	L2	$10	WIN	$10	$82	$0
34	W1	$5	L	($5)	$77	($5)
35	L2	$10	WIN	$10	$87	$0
36	W1	$5	L	($5)	$82	($5)
37	L2	$10	WIN	$10	$92	$0
38	W1	$5	L	($5)	$87	($5)
39	L2	$10	L	($10)	$77	($15)
40	L3	$22	WIN	$22	$99	$0
41	W1	$5	WIN	$5	$104	$0
42	W2	$5	L	($5)	$99	($5)
43	L2	$10	L	($10)	$89	($15)
44	L3	$22	WIN	$22	$111	$0
45	W1	$5	PUSH	$0	$111	$0
46	W1	$5	WIN	$5	$116	$0
47	W2	$5	L	($5)	$111	($5)
48	L2	$10	PUSH	$0	$111	($5)
49	L2	$10	L	($10)	$101	($15)
50	L3	$22	L	($22)	$79	($37)
51	L4	$46	WIN	$46	$125	$0
52	W1	$5	WIN	$5	$130	$0
53	W2	$5	L	($5)	$125	($5)
54	L2	$10	WIN	$10	$135	$0
55	W1	$5	L	($5)	$130	($5)
56	L2	$10	L	($10)	$120	($15)
57	L3	$22	WIN	$22	$142	$0
58	W1	$5	WIN	$5	$147	$0
59	W2	$5	PUSH	$0	$147	$0
60	W2	$5	PUSH	$0	$147	$0
61	W2	$5	L	($5)	$142	($5)
62	L2	$10	L	($10)	$132	($15)
63	L3	$22	L	($22)	$110	($37)
64	L4	$46	L	($46)	$64	($83)
65	L5	$5	WIN	$5	$69	($78)
66	W5 CLB1	$30	WIN	$30	$99	$0

HAND NO.	BET CODE	BET AMT	RESULT	GAIN/ LOSS	RUNNING BALANCE	CLB ACCRUAL
67	W1	$5	WIN	$5	$104	$0
68	W2	$5	L	($5)	$99	($5)
69	L2	$10	L	($10)	$89	($15)
70	L3	$22	L	($22)	$67	($37)
71	L4	$46	WIN	$46	$113	$0
72	W1	$5	WIN	$5	$118	$0
73	W2	$5	L	($5)	$113	($5)
74	L2	$10	L	($10)	$103	($15)
75	L3	$22	WIN	$22	$125	$0
76	W1	$5	WIN	$5	$130	$0
77	W2	$5	L	($5)	$125	($5)
78	L2	$10	WIN	$10	$135	$0
79	W1	$5	L	($5)	$130	($5)
80	L2	$10	WIN	$10	$140	$0
81	W1	$5	L	($5)	$135	($5)
82	L2	$10	L	($10)	$125	($15)
83	L3	$22	L	($22)	$103	($37)
84	L4	$46	L	($46)	$57	($83)
85	L5	$5	L	($5)	$52	($88)
86	L5	$5	L	($5)	$47	($93)
87	L5	$5	L	($5)	$42	($98)
88	L5	$5	PUSH	$0	$42	($98)
89	L5	$5	WIN	$5	$47	($93)
90	W5 CLB1	$35	WIN	$35	$82	$0
91	W1	$5	L	($5)	$77	($5)
92	L2	$10	WIN	$10	$87	$0
93	W1	$5	PUSH	$0	$87	$0
94	W1	$5	WIN	$5	$92	$0
95	W2	$5	WIN	$5	$97	$0
96	W3	$8	L	($8)	$89	($8)
97	L2	$10	WIN	$10	$99	$0
98	W1	$5	L	($5)	$94	($5)
99	L2	$10	WIN	$10	$104	$0
100	W1	$5	WIN	$5	$109	$0

HAND NO.	BET CODE	BET AMT	RESULT	GAIN/ LOSS	RUNNING BALANCE	CLB ACCRUAL
101	W2	$5	L	($5)	$104	($5)
102	L2	$10	L	($10)	$94	($15)
103	L3	$22	L	($22)	$72	($37)
104	L4	$46	PUSH	$0	$72	($37)
105	L4	$46	WIN	$46	$118	$0
106	W1	$5	L	($5)	$113	($5)
107	L2	$10	PUSH	$0	$113	($5)
108	L2	$10	L	($10)	$103	($15)
109	L3	$22	WIN	$22	$125	$0
110	W1	$5	L	($5)	$120	($5)
111	L2	$10	WIN	$10	$130	$0
112	W1	$5	WIN	$5	$135	$0
113	W2	$5	WIN	$5	$140	$0
114	W3	$8	L	($8)	$132	($8)
115	L2	$10	WIN	$10	$142	$0
116	W1	$5	L	($5)	$137	($5)
117	L2	$10	WIN	$10	$147	$0
118	W1	$5	WIN	$5	$152	$0
119	W2	$5	L	($5)	$147	($5)
120	L2	$10	L	($10)	$137	($15)
121	L3	$22	WIN	$22	$159	$0
122	W1	$5	WIN	$5	$164	$0
123	W2	$5	L	($5)	$159	($5)
124	L2	$10	L	($10)	$149	($15)
125	L3	$22	WIN	$22	$171	$0
126	W1	$5	L	($5)	$166	($5)
127	L2	$10	WIN	$10	$176	$0
128	W1	$5	L	($5)	$171	($5)
129	L2	$10	L	($10)	$161	($15)
130	L3	$22	L	($22)	$139	($37)
131	L4	$46	WIN	$46	$185	$0
132	W1	$5	L	($5)	$180	($5)
133	L2	$10	WIN	$10	$190	$0
134	W1	$5	WIN	$5	$195	$0

HAND NO.	BET CODE	BET AMT	RESULT	GAIN/ LOSS	RUNNING BALANCE	CLB ACCRUAL
135	W2	$5	L	($5)	$190	($5)
136	L2	$10	L	($10)	$180	($15)
137	L3	$22	L	($22)	$158	($37)
138	L4	$46	WIN	$46	$204	$0
139	W1	$5	L	($5)	$199	($5)
140	L2	$10	L	($10)	$189	($15)
141	L3	$22	L	($22)	$167	($37)
142	L4	$46	L	($46)	$121	($83)
143	L5	$5	WIN	$5	$126	($78)
144	W5 CLB1	$30	WIN	$30	$156	$0
145	W1	$5	WIN	$5	$161	$0
146	W2	$5	L	($5)	$156	($5)
147	L2	$10	WIN	$10	$166	$0
148	W1	$5	L	($5)	$161	($5)
149	L2	$10	WIN	$10	$171	$0
150	W1	$5	WIN	$5	$176	$0
151	W2	$5	L	($5)	$171	($5)
152	L2	$10	PUSH	$0	$171	($5)
153	L2	$10	L	($10)	$161	($15)
154	L3	$22	L	($22)	$139	($37)
155	L4	$46	WIN	$46	$185	$0
156	W1	$5	L	($5)	$180	($5)
157	L2	$10	WIN	$10	$190	$0
158	W1	$5	WIN	$5	$195	$0
159	W2	$5	L	($5)	$190	($5)
160	L2	$10	L	($10)	$180	($18)

SESSION STATISTICS

CLB LEVEL 1	**40%**
CLB LEVEL 2	0%
CLB LEVEL 3	0%
Goal for the session	**$90**
Estimated hands per hour	100
Maximum table limit	$500

Highest bet made in the entire series	**$46**
What hand did we make that bet?	11
What was the balance at that time?	($23)

Highest balance achieved	**$204**
At what hand?	138

Lowest balance experienced	**($23)**
At what hand?	10

Goal amount achieved	**$92**
At what hand achieved?	**37**
Minutes required to achieve goal	22.2
Dollars wagered to reach the goal	$401
Total R.O.I. upon reaching goal	**22.94%**

Ending Series Balance	**$180**
Total dollars wagered in the entire series	$1,954
Total R.O.I. - the entire series	**9.21%**

No. of CLB-L1 bets to reach goal?	0
No. of CLB-L2 bets to reach goal?	0
No. of CLB-L3 bets to reach goal?	0

No. of CLB-L1 bets in the entire series?	**3**
No. of CLB-L2 bets in the entire series?	0
No. of CLB-L3 bets in the entire series?	0

43.13%	**WINS**	69
48.75%	**LOSSES**	78
8.13%	**PUSHES**	13
100.00%	**TOTAL**	**160**

FIGURE 9-6

First, the CLB bets are coded in this manner: W5 CLB 1, meaning that the CLB bet occurred at bet code W5, and CLB Level 1 was computed. Now, I realize that we haven't discussed the various CLB levels yet, but those topics are coming in Chapter 10. Okay, so what do we have here in this run of 160 bets or hands? Let's take a look at some statistics.

As you review the results of Figure 9-5, you can see that we experienced a few consecutive losses before achieving our first win. This happens, and this chart is a great example of what could happen the minute you first jump in. As the statistics indicate, we lost more than we won and still we were able to win $180 using the semi-aggressive 40%-CLB model where we make the L4 $46 bet. Remember, the starting point of $0 in Figure 9-5 reflects the fact that you have the $200 of recommended buy-in money in front of you; therefore, in the running balance column, for example, on hand 160 we have profited $180, now having a total of $380 in front of us, which is the buy-in plus the profit. The big story is that we achieved our goal of eighteen units at hand 37. At a rate of two hands per minute, which by most standards is way below the average rate of dealt cards going head-to-head against the dealer, we achieved our goal in about twenty-two minutes.

Normally, we now safeguard our win by walking away and declaring that this session is over. However, here we will stay and see what happens for the eighty minutes of play to formulate the analysis. In this case we won at an equivalent rate of approximately $100 per hour, definitely well above our normal average. Important to note, as well, is that doubles and splits have *not* been factored in. If you are "casually counting" the cards you should hit at least about a 55% to 65% average in making those hands as well, which would even make the final outcome a little better. More about the casual count in Chapter 12.

Now then, let's examine where we encountered our first 40%-CLB bet and how many we experienced in the 160 hands. Okay, we go to hand 66 and see our first occurrence of a successive loss and trigger into the stage 2 CLB area. Before we started the loss sequence our running balance was a positive $147; we then began a losing sequence and lost a sum total of $78. But then we hit our 40%-CLB bet for $30 and began our road back to recovery. At hand 80 we nearly recovered with a balance of $140 and totally recovered at hand 117. Then we began the process of winning and gaining profits again. This loss event is a fact of life in this game! It will happen to you; there is no doubt. However, we dramatically curtail the opportunity of this event from happening by forcing ourselves to step out of the game once our eighteen- to twenty-unit goal is achieved. In this particular model, going into the stage 2 tier occurred only once, which is a little under the average.

Additionally, the following analysis will assist in providing insight into various betting options and tier levels that you can specifically design to accommodate the levels of play that you are comfortable betting at. For example, you may decide to absolutely terminate zone betting at bet L4 and never go to the CLB mode at all because losing that much in a series gets you nervous. Hey, that's okay—the game should be enjoyable and comfortable. Be assured that you *will* win the money; just realize that the more aggressive you are, the quicker the results.

It's important to note that you should never bet unit sizes that make you uncomfortable. This is key because there are times when you must make some adjustments in the amount of betting positions you are playing, and if your bet unit is too high, you may get really uncomfortable betting that kind of money. For example, in switching from one hand to two hands most casinos require you to double the table minimum to play; thus, if you are betting $5 units and want to play two hands, you now have to bet $10 per position or $20 total each time, which may make you extremely uncomfortable. If you decide to do this (and in some cases you may have to!), then remember your session money has to be modeled for this kind of betting as well. If you are determined to bet two positions I can't emphasize enough that you need the bankroll with you to sustain that effort, not to mention that now you have to separately track two hands independently, which can be difficult if you haven't established a system for doing so. An easy way to get around having to double your unit size to play two positions is having a friend place the bets for you on the second position under your direction. As far as the casino is concerned there are two people playing two positions so the technical requirement has been satisfied.

Besides the initial losses, several other important factors can be seen at the bottom of Figure 9-6. I view making bets similar to making investments—everyone wants a return on investment (R.O.I.), right? Well, each time you make a bet you are investing for a possible positive outcome. Granted, this is the most risky investment you can make, but as Figure 9-6 indicates, after all the bets or investments or wagers have been made to the tune of $401, we are still able to show an R.O.I. of $92 (22.94%) at hand 37. This is optimum considering there were more losing hands than winning ones (to the tune of 13% more), which is very uncharacteristic of what the outcome usually is; generally the outcome should be a little closer to fifty-one hands won for the house versus forty-nine in favor of the player, not factoring in for pushed hands which are usually 8% to 12% of all hands played. Additionally, the overall increase in cash is 90%, over the initial session (buy-in) money for the 160 hands played. Needless to say this strategy does work. We were able to withstand a reasonably long loss and recover in fifty-two hands of play or in about thirty minutes.

Keeping Track of Your CLB

Another issue that you may be wondering about is how to keep track of the CLB? Well, it's pretty easy, actually. When you buy in at the table, ask for about $30 of white $1 chips. When you begin a loss sequence, place one chip off the stack into its own stack for every $5 lost, and begin another stack for the dollar units lost. For example, if you lose an $8 bet, you would place one chip next to the railing of the table (this represents one unit of $5) and three chips stacked together right next to it (this represents the $3 extra to make eight). Each time you lose a bet, you stack these chips on top of one another. If you lose a $24 bet, you would place four white chips on the $5 stack and four white chips on the $1 stack, and so on. Thus, when having to make a CLB bet you merely look at both stacks and you have an accurate tally of the aggregate sum total of the sequence loss and can make your percentage bet accurately.

Modifying and Creating Your Own Betting Strategy

As I indicated in the introduction of this book, my intent is to assist you in analyzing some important facts about the game that usually most folks don't pay attention to. You have just analyzed one of the really big ones! Now then, having this information enables you to modify and create your own betting strategy that you can be comfortable with. If the CLB method appeals to you, then make a model that fits your playing acumen. There are more samples of this strategy coming later in this chapter, and they all have their place because sometimes you may want to switch to different strategies in any one session, depending on what the cards are doing, to again suit your betting comfort levels. But the great thing is, the strategy works! And what I said earlier about most of the action occurring in the zone is validated. If you look at the outcomes, you'll quickly see that 80% of the action stays between bets W1 through W4 on the win side, and bets L1 through L4 on the loss side. Modifying the bet levels to suit your needs is totally up to you. By looking at Figure 9-6, you can see we've accomplished the goal that we sought:

- Loss recovery
- Wining eighteen to twenty units in an acceptable time frame

At this point you may be thinking, "What about a more conservative strategy where I don't have to bet so high when I lose?" Using the same CLB strategy you can streamline your betting by extending or shortening your own zone. This doesn't change the actual probability of where the real zone actually is, but rather allows you to extend or shorten your loss sequences by either tweaking (1) the percentage of CLB, or (2) the amount of bets made before going to stage 2, or (3) the size of the bets while in the zone.

Let's look at a strategy that *may* seem more realistic to some of you. Refer to the CLB strategy shown in Figure 9-3 and let's see what kind of impact lowering the bets while staying in the zone has on the overall picture. We'll outline the same 160-hand run once more and show the associated statistics.

FIGURE 9-7
RANDOM RUN FOR (160) RESULTS — $5 BET UNITS — MODEL 2

HAND NO.	BET CODE	BET AMT	RESULT	GAIN/ LOSS	RUNNING BALANCE	CLB ACCRUAL
INITIAL	W1	$5	PUSH	$0	$0	$0
2	W1	$5	L	($5)	($5)	($5)
3	L2	$10	L	($10)	($15)	($15)
4	L3	$15	WIN	$15	$0	$0
5	W1	$5	WIN	$5	$5	$0
6	W2	$5	WIN	$5	$10	$0
7	W3	$8	L	($8)	$2	($8)
8	L2	$10	L	($10)	($8)	($18)
9	L3	$15	PUSH	$0	($8)	($18)
10	L3	$15	L	($15)	($23)	($33)
11	L4	$25	PUSH	$0	($23)	($33)
12	L4	$25	WIN	$25	$2	$0
13	W1	$5	WIN	$5	$7	$0
14	W2	$5	L	($5)	$2	($5)
15	L2	$10	L	($10)	($8)	($15)
16	L3	$15	WIN	$15	$7	$0
17	W1	$5	WIN	$5	$12	$0
18	W2	$5	L	($5)	$7	($5)
19	L2	$10	WIN	$10	$17	$0
20	W1	$5	L	($5)	$12	($5)
21	L2	$10	WIN	$10	$22	$0
22	W1	$5	WIN	$5	$27	$0
23	W2	$5	L	($5)	$22	($5)
24	L2	$10	WIN	$10	$32	$0
25	W1	$5	L	($5)	$27	($5)
26	L2	$10	WIN	$10	$37	$0
27	W1	$5	WIN	$5	$42	$0
28	W2	$5	WIN	$5	$47	$0
29	W3	$8	L	($8)	$39	($8)
30	L2	$10	WIN	$10	$49	$0
31	W1	$5	L	($5)	$44	($5)
32	L2	$10	PUSH	$0	$44	($5)

HAND NO.	BET CODE	BET AMT	RESULT	GAIN/ LOSS	RUNNING BALANCE	CLB ACCRUAL
33	L2	$10	WIN	$10	$54	$0
34	W1	$5	L	($5)	$49	($5)
35	L2	$10	WIN	$10	$59	$0
36	W1	$5	L	($5)	$54	($5)
37	L2	$10	WIN	$10	$64	$0
38	W1	$5	L	($5)	$59	($5)
39	L2	$10	L	($10)	$49	($15)
40	L3	$15	WIN	$15	$64	$0
41	W1	$5	WIN	$5	$69	$0
42	W2	$5	L	($5)	$64	($5)
43	L2	$10	L	($10)	$54	($15)
44	L3	$15	WIN	$15	$69	$0
45	W1	$5	PUSH	$0	$69	$0
46	W1	$5	WIN	$5	$74	$0
47	W2	$5	L	($5)	$69	($5)
48	L2	$10	PUSH	$0	$69	($5)
49	L2	$10	L	($10)	$59	($15)
50	L3	$15	L	($15)	$44	($30)
51	L4	$25	WIN	$25	$69	$0
52	W1	$5	WIN	$5	$74	$0
53	W2	$5	L	($5)	$69	($5)
54	L2	$10	WIN	$10	$79	$0
55	W1	$5	L	($5)	$74	($5)
56	L2	$10	L	($10)	$64	($15)
57	L3	$15	WIN	$15	$79	$0
58	W1	$5	WIN	$5	$84	$0
59	W2	$5	PUSH	$0	$84	$0
60	W2	$5	PUSH	$0	$84	$0
61	W2	$5	L	($5)	$79	($5)
62	L2	$10	L	($10)	$69	($15)
63	L3	$15	L	($15)	$54	($30)
64	L4	$25	L	($25)	$29	($55)
65	L5	$5	WIN	$5	$34	($50)
66	W5 CLB1	$20	WIN	$20	$54	$0

HAND NO.	BET CODE	BET AMT	RESULT	GAIN/ LOSS	RUNNING BALANCE	CLB ACCRUAL
67	W1	$5	WIN	$5	$59	$0
68	W2	$5	L	($5)	$54	($5)
69	L2	$10	L	($10)	$44	($15)
70	L3	$15	L	($15)	$29	($30)
71	L4	$25	WIN	$25	$54	$0
72	W1	$5	WIN	$5	$59	$0
73	W2	$5	L	($5)	$54	($5)
74	L2	$10	L	($10)	$44	($15)
75	L3	$15	WIN	$15	$59	$0
76	W1	$5	WIN	$5	$64	$0
77	W2	$5	L	($5)	$59	($5)
78	L2	$10	WIN	$10	$69	$0
79	W1	$5	L	($5)	$64	($5)
80	L2	$10	WIN	$10	$74	$0
81	W1	$5	L	($5)	$69	($5)
82	L2	$10	L	($10)	$59	($15)
83	L3	$15	L	($15)	$44	($30)
84	L4	$25	L	($25)	$19	($55)
85	L5	$5	L	($5)	$14	($60)
86	L5	$5	L	($5)	$9	($65)
87	L5	$5	L	($5)	$4	($70)
88	L5	$5	PUSH	$0	$4	($70)
89	L5	$5	WIN	$5	$9	($65)
90	W5 CLB1	$25	WIN	$25	$34	$0
91	W1	$5	L	($5)	$29	($5)
92	L2	$10	WIN	$10	$39	$0
93	W1	$5	PUSH	$0	$39	$0
94	W1	$5	WIN	$5	$44	$0
95	W2	$5	WIN	$5	$49	$0
96	W3	$8	L	($8)	$41	($8)
97	L2	$10	WIN	$10	$51	$0
98	W1	$5	L	($5)	$46	($5)
99	L2	$10	WIN	$10	$56	$0
100	W1	$5	WIN	$5	$61	$0

HAND NO.	BET CODE	BET AMT	RESULT	GAIN/ LOSS	RUNNING BALANCE	CLB ACCRUAL
101	W2	$5	L	($5)	$56	($5)
102	L2	$10	L	($10)	$46	($15)
103	L3	$15	L	($15)	$31	($30)
104	L4	$25	PUSH	$0	$31	($30)
105	L4	$25	WIN	$25	$56	$0
106	W1	$5	L	($5)	$51	($5)
107	L2	$10	PUSH	$0	$51	($5)
108	L2	$10	L	($10)	$41	($15)
109	L3	$15	WIN	$15	$56	$0
110	W1	$5	L	($5)	$51	($5)
111	L2	$10	WIN	$10	$61	$0
112	W1	$5	WIN	$5	$66	$0
113	W2	$5	WIN	$5	$71	$0
114	W3	$8	L	($8)	$63	($8)
115	L2	$10	WIN	$10	$73	$0
116	W1	$5	L	($5)	$68	($5)
117	L2	$10	WIN	$10	$78	$0
118	W1	$5	WIN	$5	$83	$0
119	W2	$5	L	($5)	$78	($5)
120	L2	$10	L	($10)	$68	($15)
121	L3	$15	WIN	$15	$83	$0
122	W1	$5	WIN	$5	$88	$0
123	W2	$5	L	($5)	$83	($5)
124	L2	$10	L	($10)	$73	($15)
125	L3	$15	WIN	$15	$88	$0
126	W1	$5	L	($5)	$83	($5)
127	L2	$10	WIN	$10	$93	$0
128	W1	$5	L	($5)	$88	($5)
129	L2	$10	L	($10)	$78	($15)
130	L3	$15	L	($15)	$63	($30)
131	L4	$25	WIN	$25	$88	$0
132	W1	$5	L	($5)	$83	($5)
133	L2	$10	WIN	$10	$93	$0
134	W1	$5	WIN	$5	$98	$0

HAND NO.	BET CODE	BET AMT	RESULT	GAIN/ LOSS	RUNNING BALANCE	CLB ACCRUAL
135	W2	$5	L	($5)	$93	($5)
136	L2	$10	L	($10)	$83	($15)
137	L3	$15	L	($15)	$68	($30)
138	L4	$25	WIN	$25	$93	$0
139	W1	$5	L	($5)	$88	($5)
140	L2	$10	L	($10)	$78	($15)
141	L3	$15	L	($15)	$63	($30)
142	L4	$25	L	($25)	$38	($55)
143	L5	$5	WIN	$5	$43	($50)
144	W5 CLB1	$20	WIN	$20	$63	$0
145	W1	$5	WIN	$5	$68	$0
146	W2	$5	L	($5)	$63	($5)
147	L2	$10	WIN	$10	$73	$0
148	W1	$5	L	($5)	$68	($5)
149	L2	$10	WIN	$10	$78	$0
150	W1	$5	WIN	$5	$83	$0
151	W2	$5	L	($5)	$78	($5)
152	L2	$10	PUSH	$0	$78	($5)
153	L2	$10	L	($10)	$68	($15)
154	L3	$15	L	($15)	$53	($30)
155	L4	$25	WIN	$25	$78	$0
156	W1	$5	L	($5)	$73	($5)
157	L2	$10	WIN	$10	$83	$0
158	W1	$5	WIN	$5	$88	$0
159	W2	$5	L	($5)	$83	($5)
160	L2	$10	L	($10)	$73	($18)

SESSION STATISTICS

CLB LEVEL 1	40%
CLB LEVEL 2	0%
CLB LEVEL 3	0%
Goal for the session	**$90**
Estimated hands per hour	100
Maximum table limit	$500

Highest bet made in the entire series	**$25.00**
What hand did we make that bet?	11
What was the balance at that time?	($23)

Highest balance achieved	**$98**
At what hand?	134

Lowest balance experienced	**($23)**
At what hand?	10

Goal amount achieved	**$93**
At what hand achieved?	**127**
Minutes required to achieve goal	76.2
Dollars wagered to reach the goal	$1,182
Total R.O.I. upon reaching goal	**7.87%**

Ending Series Balance	**$73**
Total dollars wagered in the entire series	$1,532
Total R.O.I. - the entire series	**4.77%**

No. of CLB-L1 bets to reach goal?	**2**
No. of CLB-L2 bets to reach goal?	0
No. of CLB-L3 bets to reach goal?	0

No. of CLB-L1 bets in the entire series?	**3**
No. of CLB-L2 bets in the entire series?	0
No. of CLB-L3 bets in the entire series?	0

43.13%	**WINS**	69
48.75%	**LOSSES**	78
8.13%	**PUSHES**	13
100.00%	**TOTAL**	**160**

FIGURE 9-8

After looking at the figures, we immediately see that lowering the bets definitely lowers our potential for greater profits. We reached our goal of eighteen to twenty units at hand 127, which is almost at our eighty-minute marker, and the most money won was at hand 134 for a total of $98. So what can we conclude from this? The problem is that bet L2 certainly *does* cover the loss experienced in the win column at either the $5 or $8 levels, but bet L3 *does not* cover the loss from the win column and the L2 bet, when the L2 bet is $8. Additionally, if the loss goes to L4, then the L4 bet covers only the L3 and L2 bets, and does not cover the loss experienced in the win column that initiated the entire loss sequence of betting. This places you continually in a deficit situation looking for additional wins, splits, double downs, and blackjacks to make up the difference. We can surmise that when we lower the betting parameters, we must adjust the unit goal we'd like to achieve and possibly lower it by 40% to 50%! So, instead of seeking an eighteen- to twenty-unit goal, we go for a nine- to ten-unit goal.

In the following figure, we can see exactly what happens under the same conditions if we change the goal. We won't display the entire run; we just changed the goal parameters. The important thing here is to understand that through this analysis and the others presented, you can clearly see why setting a unit goal is so critical, because it makes you a winner every time! As we look at Figure 9-9, it's all pretty predictable what will happen!

SESSION STATISTICS

CLB LEVEL 1	**40%**
CLB LEVEL 2	0%
CLB LEVEL 3	0%
Goal for the session	**$50**
Estimated hands per hour	100
Maximum table limit	$500

Highest bet made in the entire series	**$25**
What hand did we make that bet?	11
What was the balance at that time?	($23)

Highest balance achieved	**$98**
At what hand?	134

Lowest balance experienced	**($23)**
At what hand?	10

Goal amount achieved	**$54**
At what hand achieved?	**33**
Minutes required to achieve goal	19.8
Dollars wagered to reach the goal	$301
Total R.O.I. upon reaching goal	**17.94%**

Ending Series Balance	**$73**
Total dollars wagered in the entire series	$1,532
Total R.O.I. - the entire series	**4.77%**

No. of CLB-L1 bets to reach goal?	0
No. of CLB-L2 bets to reach goal?	0
No. of CLB-L3 bets to reach goal?	0

No. of CLB-L1 bets in the entire series?	**3**
No. of CLB-L2 bets in the entire series?	0
No. of CLB-L3 bets in the entire series?	0

43.13%	**WINS**	69
48.75%	**LOSSES**	78
8.13%	**PUSHES**	13
100.00%	**TOTAL**	**160**

FIGURE 9-9

There are some things in Figure 9-9 that correlate well to what we've been analyzing, and that is, there are a little fewer profit dollars at the end of the series because there is less risk involved. This is a correlation we haven't discussed yet, but is readily apparent in the analysis of the CLB factor change. Ultimately, when going into a reduced percentage CLB mode, it *does* makes sense that, if we are making smaller percentage recovery bets, something has to give way—either the total amount achieved at the end of the 160 hands will be lower or the time required and the number of hands that need to be played need to be extended to reach a higher goal. It's just that simple! Since the rule that says "the longer you stay at the tables, the greater the opportunity to get ground out by the casino" is a definite reality, you must carefully weigh the factors by asking yourself these questions: Do I want to hang out and just play some cards at my ease for a few hours, or do I want to get in and' get out with a quick profit? Only *you* can answer those questions!

Increasing the CLB Factor—The Percentage of Recovery

I'm sure that at this point most of you are wondering what would happen if we increased the percentage rate of recovery in our CLB factor, right? Here we'll end your curiosity. Obviously, before we get started we know a couple things— the recovery bets will be higher, the output model is the same, and therefore our ending profits will be higher. But what else? How about we might possibly reach our goal sooner?

The statistics in Figure 9-10 are generated for the strategy shown in Figure 9-2, cranking up the CLB factor to 60%; nothing else was changed. Run the comparison between the statistics in Figure 9-6 (the original run), and the ones in Figure 9-10, and the results are pretty interesting. We reset our goal for eighteen to twenty units.

SESSION STATISTICS

CLB LEVEL 1	60%
CLB LEVEL 2	0%
CLB LEVEL 3	0%
Goal for the session	**$90**
Estimated hands per hour	100
Maximum table limit	$500

Highest bet made in the entire series	**$55**
What hand did we make that bet?	90
What was the balance at that time?	$62

Highest balance achieved	**$245**
At what hand?	158

Lowest balance experienced	**($23)**
At what hand?	10

Goal amount achieved	**$92**
At what hand achieved?	**37**
Minutes required to achieve goal	22.2
Dollars wagered to reach the goal	$401
Total R.O.I. upon reaching goal	**22.94%**

Ending Series Balance	**$230**
Total dollars wagered in the entire series	$2,004
Total R.O.I. - the entire series	**11.48%**

No. of CLB-L1 bets to reach goal?	0
No. of CLB-L2 bets to reach goal?	0
No. of CLB-L3 bets to reach goal?	0

No. of CLB-L1 bets in the entire series?	**3**
No. of CLB-L2 bets in the entire series?	0
No. of CLB-L3 bets in the entire series?	0

43.13%	**WINS**	69
48.75%	**LOSSES**	78
8.13%	**PUSHES**	13
100.00%	**TOTAL**	**160**

FIGURE 9-10

SESSION STATISTICS

CLB LEVEL 1	80%
CLB LEVEL 2	0%
CLB LEVEL 3	0%
Goal for the session	**$90**
Estimated hands per hour	100
Maximum table limit	$500

Highest bet made in the entire series	**$75**
What hand did we make that bet?	90
What was the balance at that time?	$77

Highest balance achieved	**$295**
At what hand?	158

Lowest balance experienced	**($23)**
At what hand?	10

Goal amount achieved	**$92**
At what hand achieved?	**37**
Minutes required to achieve goal	22.2
Dollars wagered to reach the goal	$401
Total R.O.I. upon reaching goal	**22.94%**

Ending Series Balance	**$280**
Total dollars wagered in the entire series	$2,054
Total R.O.I. - the entire series	**13.63%**

No. of CLB-L1 bets to reach goal?	0
No. of CLB-L2 bets to reach goal?	0
No. of CLB-L3 bets to reach goal?	0

No. of CLB-L1 bets in the entire series?	**3**
No. of CLB-L2 bets in the entire series?	0
No. of CLB-L3 bets in the entire series?	0

43.13%	**WINS**	69
48.75%	**LOSSES**	78
8.13%	**PUSHES**	13
100.00%	**TOTAL**	**160**

FIGURE 9-11

As you can see, we again met our goal at hand 37. Additionally, our ending series balance is greater; we went from $180 to $245 and our overall R.O.I. is higher as well. But the big bonus is our totally recovery of our first CLB at hand 78, which is only seventeen hands from where the loss sequence was initiated. Also, the highest bet went from $46 to $55, which is nominal.

So, we will perform one last comparison in Figure 9-11, elevating the CLB from 60% to 80% using the same comparison to Figure 9-2.

As you can see, our highest bet now goes from $55 to $75, up almost $30 from the original $46. Our ending series total went from $245 to $280, again increasing our overall R.O.I. from 11.48% to 13.63%, definitely not worth the additional risk, in my opinion.

Extending the Zone to One More Winning or Losing Bet

I'm often asked by some of my seminar students why I don't extend the zone to one more bet. It's definitely okay to do that, but there are many downsides. For instance, you have to make adjustments to your session money and overall bankroll, moving them up a bit to withstand higher betting limits. Additionally, you need a little more nerve to make a go of it. In Figure 9-12 we extend the zone for Model-1, which now morphs into Model-3, to see what it might look like.

We can readily see in Figure 9-12 that bet L5 covers losses in L4 plus L3 and L2 with no profit, but doesn't cover any loss from the win column, which again initiates any loss sequence. You can adjust this type of betting scenario any way you'd like. The idea behind going one more bet in extending the zone is to prevent the need to go into CLB mode betting. Take a look at Figures 9-13 and 9-14 and let's see what happens with the same results run from the previous models, this time using a 40-CLB factor.

CLB STRATEGY - MODEL 3
Aggressive EXTENDED CLB-ZONE Stage Betting
(For a $5 Minimum Table and/or Base Unit size)

Tier Level Betting WIN Schema

Bet Code	Bet Amount	Double or Split OK	Chance of a Player Win	IF WIN GO TO	IF LOSS GO TO
THE ZONE					
W1	$5	Yes	12.500%	W2	L2
W2	$5	Yes	12.500%	W3	L2
W3	$8	Yes	9.375%	W4	L2
W4	$5	Yes	6.250%	W5	L2
W5	$8	Yes	3.906%	W4	L2
CLB STAGE 2					
W6	40-CLB	No	12.500%	W1	L7
W7	40-CLB	No	12.500%	W8	L8
W8	40-CLB	No	12.500%	W8	L8
CLB STAGE 3 - OPTIONAL					
W9	$10	Yes	12.500%	W10	L2
W10	$8	Yes	12.500%	W11	L2
W11	$5	Yes	9.375%	W1	L1

Tier Level Betting LOSS Schema

Bet Code	Bet Amount	Double or Split OK	Chance of a Dealer Win	WHEN WIN GO TO	IF LOSS GO TO
THE ZONE					
L1	$5	Yes	12.500%	W1	L2
L2	$10	Yes	12.500%	W1	L3
L3	$22	No	9.375%	W1	L4
L4	$46	No	6.250%	W1	L5
L5	$78	No	3.906%	W1	L6
CLB STAGE 2					
L6	$5	Yes	Variable	W6	L6
L7	$5	Yes	Variable	W7	L7
L8	$5	Yes	Variable	W8	L8

FIGURE 9-12

FIGURE 9-13
RANDOM RUN FOR (160) RESULTS — $5 BET UNITS — MODEL 3

HAND NO.	BET CODE	BET AMT	RESULT	GAIN/ LOSS	RUNNING BALANCE	CLB ACCRUAL
INITIAL	W1	$5	PUSH	$0	$0	$0
2	W1	$5	L	($5)	($5)	($5)
3	L2	$10	L	($10)	($15)	($15)
4	L3	$22	WIN	$22	$7	$0
5	W1	$5	WIN	$5	$12	$0
6	W2	$5	WIN	$5	$17	$0
7	W3	$8	L	($8)	$9	($8)
8	L2	$10	L	($10)	($1)	($18)
9	L3	$22	PUSH	$0	($1)	($18)
10	L3	$22	L	($22)	($23)	($40)
11	L4	$46	PUSH	$0	($23)	($40)
12	L4	$46	WIN	$46	$23	$0
13	W1	$5	WIN	$5	$28	$0
14	W2	$5	L	($5)	$23	($5)
15	L2	$10	L	($10)	$13	($15)
16	L3	$22	WIN	$22	$35	$0
17	W1	$5	WIN	$5	$40	$0
18	W2	$5	L	($5)	$35	($5)
19	L2	$10	WIN	$10	$45	$0
20	W1	$5	L	($5)	$40	($5)
21	L2	$10	WIN	$10	$50	$0
22	W1	$5	WIN	$5	$55	$0
23	W2	$5	L	($5)	$50	($5)
24	L2	$10	WIN	$10	$60	$0
25	W1	$5	L	($5)	$55	($5)
26	L2	$10	WIN	$10	$65	$0
27	W1	$5	WIN	$5	$70	$0
28	W2	$5	WIN	$5	$75	$0
29	W3	$8	L	($8)	$67	($8)
30	L2	$10	WIN	$10	$77	$0
31	W1	$5	L	($5)	$72	($5)
32	L2	$10	PUSH	$0	$72	($5)

HAND NO.	BET CODE	BET AMT	RESULT	GAIN/ LOSS	RUNNING BALANCE	CLB ACCRUAL
33	L2	$10	WIN	$10	$82	$0
34	W1	$5	L	($5)	$77	($5)
35	L2	$10	WIN	$10	$87	$0
36	W1	$5	L	($5)	$82	($5)
37	L2	$10	WIN	$10	$92	$0
38	W1	$5	L	($5)	$87	($5)
39	L2	$10	L	($10)	$77	($15)
40	L3	$22	WIN	$22	$99	$0
41	W1	$5	WIN	$5	$104	$0
42	W2	$5	L	($5)	$99	($5)
43	L2	$10	L	($10)	$89	($15)
44	L3	$22	WIN	$22	$111	$0
45	W1	$5	PUSH	$0	$111	$0
46	W1	$5	WIN	$5	$116	$0
47	W2	$5	L	($5)	$111	($5)
48	L2	$10	PUSH	$0	$111	($5)
49	L2	$10	L	($10)	$101	($15)
50	L3	$22	L	($22)	$79	($37)
51	L4	$46	WIN	$46	$125	$0
52	W1	$5	WIN	$5	$130	$0
53	W2	$5	L	($5)	$125	($5)
54	L2	$10	WIN	$10	$135	$0
55	W1	$5	L	($5)	$130	($5)
56	L2	$10	L	($10)	$120	($15)
57	L3	$22	WIN	$22	$142	$0
58	W1	$5	WIN	$5	$147	$0
59	W2	$5	PUSH	$0	$147	$0
60	W2	$5	PUSH	$0	$147	$0
61	W2	$5	L	($5)	$142	($5)
62	L2	$10	L	($10)	$132	($15)
63	L3	$22	L	($22)	$110	($37)
64	L4	$46	L	($46)	$64	($83)
65	L5	$78	WIN	$78	$142	$0
66	W1	$5	WIN	$5	$147	$0

HAND NO.	BET CODE	BET AMT	RESULT	GAIN/ LOSS	RUNNING BALANCE	CLB ACCRUAL
67	W2	$5	WIN	$5	$152	$0
68	W3	$8	L	($8)	$144	($8)
69	L2	$10	L	($10)	$134	($18)
70	L3	$22	L	($22)	$112	($40)
71	L4	$46	WIN	$46	$158	$0
72	W1	$5	WIN	$5	$163	$0
73	W2	$5	L	($5)	$158	($5)
74	L2	$10	L	($10)	$148	($15)
75	L3	$22	WIN	$22	$170	$0
76	W1	$5	WIN	$5	$175	$0
77	W2	$5	L	($5)	$170	($5)
78	L2	$10	WIN	$10	$180	$0
79	W1	$5	L	($5)	$175	($5)
80	L2	$10	WIN	$10	$185	$0
81	W1	$5	L	($5)	$180	($5)
82	L2	$10	L	($10)	$170	($15)
83	L3	$22	L	($22)	$148	($37)
84	L4	$46	L	($46)	$102	($83)
85	L5	$78	L	($78)	$24	($161)
86	L6	$5	L	($5)	$19	($166)
87	L6	$5	L	($5)	$14	($171)
88	L6	$5	PUSH	$0	$14	($171)
89	L6	$5	WIN	$5	$19	($166)
90	W6 CLB1	$65	WIN	$65	$84	$0
91	W1	$5	L	($5)	$79	($5)
92	L2	$10	WIN	$10	$89	$0
93	W1	$5	PUSH	$0	$89	$0
94	W1	$5	WIN	$5	$94	$0
95	W2	$5	WIN	$5	$99	$0
96	W3	$8	L	($8)	$91	($8)
97	L2	$10	WIN	$10	$101	$0
98	W1	$5	L	($5)	$96	($5)
99	L2	$10	WIN	$10	$106	$0
100	W1	$5	WIN	$5	$111	$0

HAND NO.	BET CODE	BET AMT	RESULT	GAIN/ LOSS	RUNNING BALANCE	CLB ACCRUAL
101	W2	$5	L	($5)	$106	($5)
102	L2	$10	L	($10)	$96	($15)
103	L3	$22	L	($22)	$74	($37)
104	L4	$46	PUSH	$0	$74	($37)
105	L4	$46	WIN	$46	$120	$0
106	W1	$5	L	($5)	$115	($5)
107	L2	$10	PUSH	$0	$115	($5)
108	L2	$10	L	($10)	$105	($15)
109	L3	$22	WIN	$22	$127	$0
110	W1	$5	L	($5)	$122	($5)
111	L2	$10	WIN	$10	$132	$0
112	W1	$5	WIN	$5	$137	$0
113	W2	$5	WIN	$5	$142	$0
114	W3	$8	L	($8)	$134	($8)
115	L2	$10	WIN	$10	$144	$0
116	W1	$5	L	($5)	$139	($5)
117	L2	$10	WIN	$10	$149	$0
118	W1	$5	WIN	$5	$154	$0
119	W2	$5	L	($5)	$149	($5)
120	L2	$10	L	($10)	$139	($15)
121	L3	$22	WIN	$22	$161	$0
122	W1	$5	WIN	$5	$166	$0
123	W2	$5	L	($5)	$161	($5)
124	L2	$10	L	($10)	$151	($15)
125	L3	$22	WIN	$22	$173	$0
126	W1	$5	L	($5)	$168	($5)
127	L2	$10	WIN	$10	$178	$0
128	W1	$5	L	($5)	$173	($5)
129	L2	$10	L	($10)	$163	($15)
130	L3	$22	L	($22)	$141	($37)
131	L4	$46	WIN	$46	$187	$0
132	W1	$5	L	($5)	$182	($5)
133	L2	$10	WIN	$10	$192	$0
134	W1	$5	WIN	$5	$197	$0

HAND NO.	BET CODE	BET AMT	RESULT	GAIN/ LOSS	RUNNING BALANCE	CLB ACCRUAL
135	W2	$5	L	($5)	$192	($5)
136	L2	$10	L	($10)	$182	($15)
137	L3	$22	L	($22)	$160	($37)
138	L4	$46	WIN	$46	$206	$0
139	W1	$5	L	($5)	$201	($5)
140	L2	$10	L	($10)	$191	($15)
141	L3	$22	L	($22)	$169	($37)
142	L4	$46	L	($46)	$123	($83)
143	L5	$78	WIN	$78	$201	$0
144	W1	$5	WIN	$5	$206	$0
145	W2	$5	WIN	$5	$211	$0
146	W3	$8	L	($8)	$203	($8)
147	L2	$10	WIN	$10	$213	$0
148	W1	$5	L	($5)	$208	($5)
149	L2	$10	WIN	$10	$218	$0
150	W1	$5	WIN	$5	$223	$0
151	W2	$5	L	($5)	$218	($5)
152	L2	$10	PUSH	$0	$218	($5)
153	L2	$10	L	($10)	$208	($15)
154	L3	$22	L	($22)	$186	($37)
155	L4	$46	WIN	$46	$232	$0
156	W1	$5	L	($5)	$227	($5)
157	L2	$10	WIN	$10	$237	$0
158	W1	$5	WIN	$5	$242	$0
159	W2	$5	L	($5)	$237	($5)
160	L2	$10	L	($10)	$227	($18)

SESSION STATISTICS

CLB LEVEL 1	40%
CLB LEVEL 2	0%
CLB LEVEL 3	0%
Goal for the session	**$90**
Estimated hands per hour	100
Maximum table limit	$500

Highest bet made in the entire series	**$78**
What hand did we make that bet?	65
What was the balance at that time?	$64

Highest balance achieved	**$242**
At what hand?	158

Lowest balance experienced	**($23)**
At what hand?	10

Goal amount achieved	**$92**
At what hand achieved?	**37**
Minutes required to achieve goal	22.2
Dollars wagered to reach the goal	$401
Total R.O.I. upon reaching goal	**22.94%**

Ending Series Balance	**$227**
Total dollars wagered in the entire series	$2,159
Total R.O.I. - the entire series	**10.51%**

No. of CLB-L1 bets to reach goal?	0
No. of CLB-L2 bets to reach goal?	0
No. of CLB-L3 bets to reach goal?	0

No. of CLB-L1 bets in the entire series?	**1**
No. of CLB-L2 bets in the entire series?	0
No. of CLB-L3 bets in the entire series?	0

43.13%	**WINS**	69
48.75%	**LOSSES**	78
8.13%	**PUSHES**	13
100.00%	**TOTAL**	**160**

FIGURE 9-14

We can see from this run that we still reach our goal in about the same time frame. The highest bet made goes to $78, but the real news is, the goal that we set out for—fewer CLB bets—was achieved. During the entire series we reduced the recovery bets from a total of three in previous models to just one in this analysis. The downside is that we exposed ourselves to a negative CLB balance of –$171 on bet 87, and we obviously need more than $200 in session money to cover the next bet. *Bets get really high using this methodology, so beware!* I recommend session packets of $350 to $400 to go to five losing bets, just for backup.

A Strategy to Avoid

This final analysis may seem as though it's presented too late in this chapter, but actually it isn't. To appreciate the CLB recovery methodology, we need to see what 160 hands look like when we bet $5 only when losing, and escalate and regress when we are winning. Figure 9-15 shows you what the strategy looks like, and Figure 9-16 presents the 160-hand run so you can see it in action; it's pretty enlightening. I believe this will convince you that loss recovery is essential!

STRAIGHT UNIT LOSS STRATEGY
Passive - NO CLB-ZONE Stage Betting
(For a $5 Minimum Table and/or Base Unit size)

Tier Level Betting WIN Schema

Bet Code	Bet Amount	Double or Split OK	Chance of a Player Win	IF WIN GO TO	IF LOSS GO TO
			THE ZONE		
W1	$5	Yes	12.500%	W2	L2
W2	$8	Yes	12.500%	W3	L2
W3	$5	Yes	9.375%	W4	L2
W4	$5	Yes	6.250%	W3	L2

Tier Level Betting LOSS Schema

Bet Code	Bet Amount	Double or Split OK	Chance of a Dealer Win	WHEN WIN GO TO	IF LOSS GO TO
			THE ZONE		
L1	$5	Yes	12.500%	W1	L2
L2	$5	Yes	12.500%	W1	L2

FIGURE 9-15

FIGURE 9-16

RANDOM RUN FOR (160) RESULTS — $5 BET UNITS — STRAIGHT LOSS

HAND NO.	BET CODE	BET AMT	RESULT	GAIN/ LOSS	RUNNING BALANCE	CLB ACCRUAL
INITIAL	W1	$5	PUSH	$0	$0	$0
2	W1	$5	L	($5)	($5)	($5)
3	L2	$5	L	($5)	($10)	($10)
4	L2	$5	WIN	$5	($5)	$0
5	W1	$5	WIN	$5	$0	$0
6	W2	$8	WIN	$8	$8	$0
7	W3	$5	L	($5)	$3	($5)
8	L2	$5	L	($5)	($2)	($10)
9	L2	$5	PUSH	$0	($2)	($10)
10	L2	$5	L	($5)	($7)	($15)
11	L2	$5	PUSH	$0	($7)	($15)
12	L2	$5	WIN	$5	($2)	$0
13	W1	$5	WIN	$5	$3	$0
14	W2	$8	L	($8)	($5)	($8)
15	L2	$5	L	($5)	($10)	($13)
16	L2	$5	WIN	$5	($5)	$0
17	W1	$5	WIN	$5	$0	$0
18	W2	$8	L	($8)	($8)	($8)
19	L2	$5	WIN	$5	($3)	$0
20	W1	$5	L	($5)	($8)	($5)
21	L2	$5	WIN	$5	($3)	$0
22	W1	$5	WIN	$5	$2	$0
23	W2	$8	L	($8)	($6)	($8)
24	L2	$5	WIN	$5	($1)	$0
25	W1	$5	L	($5)	($6)	($5)
26	L2	$5	WIN	$5	($1)	$0
27	W1	$5	WIN	$5	$4	$0
28	W2	$8	WIN	$8	$12	$0
29	W3	$5	L	($5)	$7	($5)
30	L2	$5	WIN	$5	$12	$0
31	W1	$5	L	($5)	$7	($5)
32	L2	$5	PUSH	$0	$7	($5)

HAND NO.	BET CODE	BET AMT	RESULT	GAIN/ LOSS	RUNNING BALANCE	CLB ACCRUAL
33	L2	$5	WIN	$5	$12	$0
34	W1	$5	L	($5)	$7	($5)
35	L2	$5	WIN	$5	$12	$0
36	W1	$5	L	($5)	$7	($5)
37	L2	$5	WIN	$5	$12	$0
38	W1	$5	L	($5)	$7	($5)
39	L2	$5	L	($5)	$2	($10)
40	L2	$5	WIN	$5	$7	$0
41	W1	$5	WIN	$5	$12	$0
42	W2	$8	L	($8)	$4	($8)
43	L2	$5	L	($5)	($1)	($13)
44	L2	$5	WIN	$5	$4	$0
45	W1	$5	PUSH	$0	$4	$0
46	W1	$5	WIN	$5	$9	$0
47	W2	$8	L	($8)	$1	($8)
48	L2	$5	PUSH	$0	$1	($8)
49	L2	$5	L	($5)	($4)	($13)
50	L2	$5	L	($5)	($9)	($18)
51	L2	$5	WIN	$5	($4)	$0
52	W1	$5	WIN	$5	$1	$0
53	W2	$8	L	($8)	($7)	($8)
54	L2	$5	WIN	$5	($2)	$0
55	W1	$5	L	($5)	($7)	($5)
56	L2	$5	L	($5)	($12)	($10)
57	L2	$5	WIN	$5	($7)	$0
58	W1	$5	WIN	$5	($2)	$0
59	W2	$8	PUSH	$0	($2)	$0
60	W2	$8	PUSH	$0	($2)	$0
61	W2	$8	L	($8)	($10)	($8)
62	L2	$5	L	($5)	($15)	($13)
63	L2	$5	L	($5)	($20)	($18)
64	L2	$5	L	($5)	($25)	($23)
65	L2	$5	WIN	$5	($20)	$0
66	W1	$5	WIN	$5	($15)	$0

HAND NO.	BET CODE	BET AMT	RESULT	GAIN/ LOSS	RUNNING BALANCE	CLB ACCRUAL
67	W2	$8	WIN	$8	($7)	$0
68	W3	$5	L	($5)	($12)	($5)
69	L2	$5	L	($5)	($17)	($10)
70	L2	$5	L	($5)	($22)	($15)
71	L2	$5	WIN	$5	($17)	$0
72	W1	$5	WIN	$5	($12)	$0
73	W2	$8	L	($8)	($20)	($8)
74	L2	$5	L	($5)	($25)	($13)
75	L2	$5	WIN	$5	($20)	$0
76	W1	$5	WIN	$5	($15)	$0
77	W2	$8	L	($8)	($23)	($8)
78	L2	$5	WIN	$5	($18)	$0
79	W1	$5	L	($5)	($23)	($5)
80	L2	$5	WIN	$5	($18)	$0
81	W1	$5	L	($5)	($23)	($5)
82	L2	$5	L	($5)	($28)	($10)
83	L2	$5	L	($5)	($33)	($15)
84	L2	$5	L	($5)	($38)	($20)
85	L2	$5	L	($5)	($43)	($25)
86	L2	$5	L	($5)	($48)	($30)
87	L2	$5	L	($5)	($53)	($35)
88	L2	$5	PUSH	$0	($53)	($35)
89	L2	$5	WIN	$5	($48)	$0
90	W1	$5	WIN	$5	($43)	$0
91	W2	$8	L	($8)	($51)	($8)
92	L2	$5	WIN	$5	($46)	$0
93	W1	$5	PUSH	$0	($46)	$0
94	W1	$5	WIN	$5	($41)	$0
95	W2	$8	WIN	$8	($33)	$0
96	W3	$5	L	($5)	($38)	($5)
97	L2	$5	WIN	$5	($33)	$0
98	W1	$5	L	($5)	($38)	($5)
99	L2	$5	WIN	$5	($33)	$0
100	W1	$5	WIN	$5	($28)	$0

HAND NO.	BET CODE	BET AMT	RESULT	GAIN/ LOSS	RUNNING BALANCE	CLB ACCRUAL
101	W2	$8	L	($8)	($36)	($8)
102	L2	$5	L	($5)	($41)	($13)
103	L2	$5	L	($5)	($46)	($18)
104	L2	$5	PUSH	$0	($46)	($18)
105	L2	$5	WIN	$5	($41)	$0
106	W1	$5	L	($5)	($46)	($5)
107	L2	$5	PUSH	$0	($46)	($5)
108	L2	$5	L	($5)	($51)	($10)
109	L2	$5	WIN	$5	($46)	$0
110	W1	$5	L	($5)	($51)	($5)
111	L2	$5	WIN	$5	($46)	$0
112	W1	$5	WIN	$5	($41)	$0
113	W2	$8	WIN	$8	($33)	$0
114	W3	$5	L	($5)	($38)	($5)
115	L2	$5	WIN	$5	($33)	$0
116	W1	$5	L	($5)	($38)	($5)
117	L2	$5	WIN	$5	($33)	$0
118	W1	$5	WIN	$5	($28)	$0
119	W2	$8	L	($8)	($36)	($8)
120	L2	$5	L	($5)	($41)	($13)
121	L2	$5	WIN	$5	($36)	$0
122	W1	$5	WIN	$5	($31)	$0
123	W2	$8	L	($8)	($39)	($8)
124	L2	$5	L	($5)	($44)	($13)
125	L2	$5	WIN	$5	($39)	$0
126	W1	$5	L	($5)	($44)	($5)
127	L2	$5	WIN	$5	($39)	$0
128	W1	$5	L	($5)	($44)	($5)
129	L2	$5	L	($5)	($49)	($10)
130	L2	$5	L	($5)	($54)	($15)
131	L2	$5	WIN	$5	($49)	$0
132	W1	$5	L	($5)	($54)	($5)
133	L2	$5	WIN	$5	($49)	$0
134	W1	$5	WIN	$5	($44)	$0

HAND NO.	BET CODE	BET AMT	RESULT	GAIN/ LOSS	RUNNING BALANCE	CLB ACCRUAL
135	W2	$8	L	($8)	($52)	($8)
136	L2	$5	L	($5)	($57)	($13)
137	L2	$5	L	($5)	($62)	($18)
138	L2	$5	WIN	$5	($57)	$0
139	W1	$5	L	($5)	($62)	($5)
140	L2	$5	L	($5)	($67)	($10)
141	L2	$5	L	($5)	($72)	($15)
142	L2	$5	L	($5)	($77)	($20)
143	L2	$5	WIN	$5	($72)	$0
144	W1	$5	WIN	$5	($67)	$0
145	W2	$8	WIN	$8	($59)	$0
146	W3	$5	L	($5)	($64)	($5)
147	L2	$5	WIN	$5	($59)	$0
148	W1	$5	L	($5)	($64)	($5)
149	L2	$5	WIN	$5	($59)	$0
150	W1	$5	WIN	$5	($54)	$0
151	W2	$8	L	($8)	($62)	($8)
152	L2	$5	PUSH	$0	($62)	($8)
153	L2	$5	L	($5)	($67)	($13)
154	L2	$5	L	($5)	($72)	($18)
155	L2	$5	WIN	$5	($67)	$0
156	W1	$5	L	($5)	($72)	($5)
157	L2	$5	WIN	$5	($67)	$0
158	W1	$5	WIN	$5	($62)	$0
159	W2	$8	L	($8)	($70)	($8)
160	L2	$5	L	($5)	($75)	($18)

It's pretty dramatic, isn't it? There's a lot of "red ink" in Figure 9-16. Even with doubling down, splitting, and special blackjack payoffs and opportunities, we won't be able to recover from the ever-increasing deficit. The longer you play this one, the deeper the hole you'll be digging for yourself. There are many folks out there who adamantly subscribe to this betting philosophy; they believe it's safe and sane to play this way! You can clearly see why casinos in all the major gambling meccas are getting bigger and fancier and love to see folks come in and use this method. Figure 9-17 shows the agonizing statistics from this run.

Again the key is recovery; without it you are lost and will ultimately lose your session money and possibly even your stake. Some folks take a negative tone and call it "chasing your money," but it isn't. Chasing money is what you do when you use straight Martingale methodology. With the CLB strategy, you're using a well-defined set of rules defining when to increase and regress your bets, based on outcome occurrences. In the next chapter we'll look at some serious variants that can be employed; again, it is important to look at these variants with the idea of possibly making changes to fit your own needs, playing acumen, and overall hand out-come distribution of wins and losses observed.

SESSION STATISTICS

CLB LEVEL 1	0%
CLB LEVEL 2	0%
CLB LEVEL 3	0%
Goal for the session	**$90**
Estimated hands per hour	100
Maximum table limit	$500

Highest bet made in the entire series	**$8**
What hand did we make that bet?	6
What was the balance at that time?	$0

Highest balance achieved	**$12**
At what hand?	28

Lowest balance experienced	**($77)**
At what hand?	142

Goal amount achieved	**NA**
At what hand achieved?	**NA**
Minutes required to achieve goal	NA
Dollars wagered to reach the goal	NA
Total R.O.I. upon reaching goal	**NA**

Ending Series Balance	**-$75**
Total dollars wagered in the entire series	$872
Total R.O.I. - the entire series	**-8.60%**

No. of CLB-L1 Bets to reach goal?	NA
No. of CLB-L2 Bets to reach goal?	NA
No. of CLB-L3 Bets to reach goal?	NA

No. of CLB-L1 bets in the entire series?	NA
No. of CLB-L2 bets in the entire series?	NA
No. of CLB-L3 bets in the entire series?	NA

43.13%	**WINS**	69
48.75%	**LOSSES**	78
8.13%	**PUSHES**	13
100.00%	**TOTAL**	**160**

FIGURE 9-17

Advanced CLB Betting Strategies and Other Variations

A t this point you should have a firm grasp of the CLB methodology, the zone, and the impact of changing various components of the CLB to adjust to your bankroll, playing acumen, and threshold of nervous tension. Now I will introduce you to the various CLB levels of implementation and how they apply to a varied series of loss betting levels.

Making Small Bets in the Zone

How can you keep your bets small, use CLB methodology, and still end up a winner? First we need to define the kind of winner you are. Do you want to win slowly and play easy for two to three hours while still making a marginal profit? Or do you want to get in and out with quick profits? Do you want to win strictly on multideck shoes, or do you prefer double- and single-deck play? These are all valid and important questions you need to answer. So let's start with Figure 10-1 and put up an example of a possible betting strategy where you enter into the CLB mode while inside the zone.

ADVANCED CLB STRATEGY - MODEL 4
Conservative CLB-ZONE Stage Betting
(For a $5 Minimum Table and/or Base Unit size)

Tier Level Betting WIN Schema

Bet Code	Bet Amount	Double or Split OK	Chance of a Player Win	IF WIN GO TO	IF LOSS GO TO
			THE ZONE		
W1	$5	Yes	12.500%	W2	L2
W2	$8	Yes	12.500%	W3	L2
W3	$5	Yes	9.375%	W4	L2
W4	$8	Yes	6.250%	W3	L2
			CLB STAGE 2		
W5	110-CLB	NO	12.500%	W1	L6
W6			BYPASSED		
W7	70-CLB	NO	12.500%	W8	L7
			CLB STAGE 3 -OPTIONAL.		
W8	$8	Yes	12.500%	W9	L2
W9	$8	Yes	12.500%	W10	L2
W10	$5	Yes	9.375%	W1	L1

Tier Level Betting LOSS Schema

Bet Code	Bet Amount	Double or Split OK	Chance of a Dealer Win	WHEN WIN GO TO	IF LOSS GO TO
			THE ZONE		
L1	$5	Yes	12.500%	W1	L2
L2	$8	Yes	12.500%	W1	L3
L3	$16	NO	9.375%	W1	L4
L4	110-CLB	NO	6.250%	W1	L5
			CLB STAGE 2		
L5	$5	Yes	Variable	W5	L5
L6	80-CLB	NO	Variable	W1	L7
L7	$5	Yes	Variable	W7	L7

FIGURE 10-1

The concept of multi-CLB levels shows up at bets L4, W5, L6, and W7. It's used to stage your opportunities for recovery while limiting your exposure to hitting repeated $5 loss bets outside the zone, getting a win, going into a CLB bet, losing, and then going back to $5 minimum bets while still looking for a back-to-back win. In such a situation you choose back-to-back CLB bets as a way of minimizing loss. The various percentage levels of CLB bet structure allow you to minimize continued exposure to large extended losses.

In Figure 10-1, I have moved the normal bet of $8 from W3 to W2. I exactly matched the L2 bet with the maximum bet in the win column. The L3 bet totally covers L2 plus the maximum bet in the win column with no profits realized; and you now make your first CLB bet at L4, which is 110% of all the previous losses. This model is designed for keeping exact pace with the losses on W1 through L3 and relying on the wins in the win column, plus the L4 bet to yield profits while in the zone.

Once you move past the L4 bet and exit the zone, you go into protection mode again at the minimum bet of $5 until you get a win. Once you trigger with a win, you try again at W5 for an 80%-CLB for the double win. If W5 loses, go to bet L6 and try again at an 80%-CLB bet. If by chance you still haven't caught a back-to-back win, drop into protection mode again at bet L7 and wait for another win. This takes you to bet W7 at another 70%-CLB bet of all losses encountered. If that loses, you go back to L7 until you achieve the back-to-back win covering 70% of all losses.

Let's do the same with the 160-hand run and see what happens (see Figure 10-2). Our goal is to make pretty small bets while in the zone; let the profits come from the wins achieved in the win column plus the L4 bet while still making our eighteen- to twenty-unit profit goal in a reasonable time frame. The great thing about this model is that if you experience the back-to-back win outside the zone, the most you'll be down is 20% to 30% of all losing bets from the start of the loss sequence, and that's a nice comeback!

FIGURE 10-2
RANDOM RUN FOR (160) RESULTS — $5 BET UNITS — MODEL 4

HAND NO.	BET CODE	BET AMT	RESULT	GAIN/ LOSS	RUNNING BALANCE	CLB ACCRUAL
INITIAL	W1	$5	PUSH	$0	$0	$0
2	W1	$5	L	($5)	($5)	($5)
3	L2	$8	L	($8)	($13)	($13)
4	L3	$16	WIN	$16	$3	$0
5	W1	$5	WIN	$5	$8	$0
6	W2	$8	WIN	$8	$16	$0
7	W3	$5	L	($5)	$11	($5)
8	L2	$8	L	($8)	$3	($13)
9	L3	$16	PUSH	$0	$3	($13)
10	L3	$16	L	($16)	($13)	($29)
11	L4 CLB1	$32	PUSH	$0	($13)	($29)
12	L4	$32	WIN	$32	$19	$0
13	W1	$5	WIN	$5	$24	$0
14	W2	$8	L	($8)	$16	($8)
15	L2	$8	L	($8)	$8	($16)
16	L3	$16	WIN	$16	$24	$0
17	W1	$5	WIN	$5	$29	$0
18	W2	$8	L	($8)	$21	($8)
19	L2	$8	WIN	$8	$29	$0
20	W1	$5	L	($5)	$24	($5)
21	L2	$8	WIN	$8	$32	$0
22	W1	$5	WIN	$5	$37	$0
23	W2	$8	L	($8)	$29	($8)
24	L2	$8	WIN	$8	$37	$0
25	W1	$5	L	($5)	$32	($5)
26	L2	$8	WIN	$8	$40	$0
27	W1	$5	WIN	$5	$45	$0
28	W2	$8	WIN	$8	$53	$0
29	W3	$5	L	($5)	$48	($5)
30	L2	$8	WIN	$8	$56	$0
31	W1	$5	L	($5)	$51	($5)
32	L2	$8	PUSH	$0	$51	($5)

HAND NO.	BET CODE	BET AMT	RESULT	GAIN/ LOSS	RUNNING BALANCE	CLB ACCRUAL
33	L2	$8	WIN	$8	$59	$0
34	W1	$5	L	($5)	$54	($5)
35	L2	$8	WIN	$8	$62	$0
36	W1	$5	L	($5)	$57	($5)
37	L2	$8	WIN	$8	$65	$0
38	W1	$5	L	($5)	$60	($5)
39	L2	$8	L	($8)	$52	($13)
40	L3	$16	WIN	$16	$68	$0
41	W1	$5	WIN	$5	$73	$0
42	W2	$8	L	($8)	$65	($8)
43	L2	$8	L	($8)	$57	($16)
44	L3	$16	WIN	$16	$73	$0
45	W1	$5	PUSH	$0	$73	$0
46	W1	$5	WIN	$5	$78	$0
47	W2	$8	L	($8)	$70	($8)
48	L2	$8	PUSH	$0	$70	($8)
49	L2	$8	L	($8)	$62	($16)
50	L3	$16	L	($16)	$46	($32)
51	L4 CLB1	$35	WIN	$35	$81	$0
52	W1	$5	WIN	$5	$86	$0
53	W2	$8	L	($8)	$78	($8)
54	L2	$8	WIN	$8	$86	$0
55	W1	$5	L	($5)	$81	($5)
56	L2	$8	L	($8)	$73	($13)
57	L3	$16	WIN	$16	$89	$0
58	W1	$5	WIN	$5	$94	$0
59	W2	$8	PUSH	$0	$94	$0
60	W2	$8	PUSH	$0	$94	$0
61	W2	$8	L	($8)	$86	($8)
62	L2	$8	L	($8)	$78	($16)
63	L3	$16	L	($16)	$62	($32)
64	L4 CLB1	$35	L	($35)	$27	($67)
65	L5	$5	WIN	$5	$32	($62)
66	W5 CLB2	$50	WIN	$50	$82	$0

HAND NO.	BET CODE	BET AMT	RESULT	GAIN/ LOSS	RUNNING BALANCE	CLB ACCRUAL
67	W1	$5	WIN	$5	$87	$0
68	W2	$8	L	($8)	$79	($8)
69	L2	$8	L	($8)	$71	($16)
70	L3	$16	L	($16)	$55	($32)
71	L4 CLB1	$35	WIN	$35	$90	$0
72	W1	$5	WIN	$5	$95	$0
73	W2	$8	L	($8)	$87	($8)
74	L2	$8	L	($8)	$79	($16)
75	L3	$16	WIN	$16	$95	$0
76	W1	$5	WIN	$5	$100	$0
77	W2	$8	L	($8)	$92	($8)
78	L2	$8	WIN	$8	$100	$0
79	W1	$5	L	($5)	$95	($5)
80	L2	$8	WIN	$8	$103	$0
81	W1	$5	L	($5)	$98	($5)
82	L2	$8	L	($8)	$90	($13)
83	L3	$16	L	($16)	$74	($29)
84	L4 CLB1	$32	L	($32)	$42	($61)
85	L5	$5	L	($5)	$37	($66)
86	L5	$5	L	($5)	$32	($71)
87	L5	$5	L	($5)	$27	($76)
88	L5	$5	PUSH	$0	$27	($76)
89	L5	$5	WIN	$5	$32	($71)
90	W5 CLB2	$57	WIN	$57	$89	$0
91	W1	$5	L	($5)	$84	($5)
92	L2	$8	WIN	$8	$92	$0
93	W1	$5	PUSH	$0	$92	$0
94	W1	$5	WIN	$5	$97	$0
95	W2	$8	WIN	$8	$105	$0
96	W3	$5	L	($5)	$100	($5)
97	L2	$8	WIN	$8	$108	$0
98	W1	$5	L	($5)	$103	($5)
99	L2	$8	WIN	$8	$111	$0
100	W1	$5	WIN	$5	$116	$0

HAND NO.	BET CODE	BET AMT	RESULT	GAIN/ LOSS	RUNNING BALANCE	CLB ACCRUAL
101	W2	$8	L	($8)	$108	($8)
102	L2	$8	L	($8)	$100	($16)
103	L3	$16	L	($16)	$84	($32)
104	L4 CLB1	$35	PUSH	$0	$84	($32)
105	L4	$35	WIN	$35	$119	$0
106	W1	$5	L	($5)	$114	($5)
107	L2	$8	PUSH	$0	$114	($5)
108	L2	$8	L	($8)	$106	($13)
109	L3	$16	WIN	$16	$122	$0
110	W1	$5	L	($5)	$117	($5)
111	L2	$8	WIN	$8	$125	$0
112	W1	$5	WIN	$5	$130	$0
113	W2	$8	WIN	$8	$138	$0
114	W3	$5	L	($5)	$133	($5)
115	L2	$8	WIN	$8	$141	$0
116	W1	$5	L	($5)	$136	($5)
117	L2	$8	WIN	$8	$144	$0
118	W1	$5	WIN	$5	$149	$0
119	W2	$8	L	($8)	$141	($8)
120	L2	$8	L	($8)	$133	($16)
121	L3	$16	WIN	$16	$149	$0
122	W1	$5	WIN	$5	$154	$0
123	W2	$8	L	($8)	$146	($8)
124	L2	$8	L	($8)	$138	($16)
125	L3	$16	WIN	$16	$154	$0
126	W1	$5	L	($5)	$149	($5)
127	L2	$8	WIN	$8	$157	$0
128	W1	$5	L	($5)	$152	($5)
129	L2	$8	L	($8)	$144	($13)
130	L3	$16	L	($16)	$128	($29)
131	L4 CLB1	$32	WIN	$32	$160	$0
132	W1	$5	L	($5)	$155	($5)
133	L2	$8	WIN	$8	$163	$0
134	W1	$5	WIN	$5	$168	$0

HAND NO.	BET CODE	BET AMT	RESULT	GAIN/ LOSS	RUNNING BALANCE	CLB ACCRUAL
135	W2	$8	L	($8)	$160	($8)
136	L2	$8	L	($8)	$152	($16)
137	L3	$16	L	($16)	$136	($32)
138	L4 CLB1	$35	WIN	$35	$171	$0
139	W1	$5	L	($5)	$166	($5)
140	L2	$8	L	($8)	$158	($13)
141	L3	$16	L	($16)	$142	($29)
142	L4 CLB1	$32	L	($32)	$110	($61)
143	L5	$5	WIN	$5	$115	($56)
144	W5 CLB2	$45	WIN	$45	$160	$0
145	W1	$5	WIN	$5	$165	$0
146	W2	$8	L	($8)	$157	($8)
147	L2	$8	WIN	$8	$165	$0
148	W1	$5	L	($5)	$160	($5)
149	L2	$8	WIN	$8	$168	$0
150	W1	$5	WIN	$5	$173	$0
151	W2	$8	L	($8)	$165	($8)
152	L2	$8	PUSH	$0	$165	($8)
153	L2	$8	L	($8)	$157	($16)
154	L3	$16	L	($16)	$141	($32)
155	L4 CLB1	$35	WIN	$35	$176	$0
156	W1	$5	L	($5)	$171	($5)
157	L2	$8	WIN	$8	$179	$0
158	W1	$5	WIN	$5	$184	$0
159	W2	$8	L	($8)	$176	($8)
160	L2	$8	L	($8)	$168	($29)

Wow, look at all those CLB bets! Yes sir, there are a lot of them, but take note that when you see an L4 CLB1 you are making a 10% profit on all the previous losses; and when you see a W5 CLB2 you are recapturing 80% of all bets lost up to that point, and that's certainly a great recovery scenario! The statistics on this run are shown in Figure 10-3.

SESSION STATISTICS

CLB LEVEL 1	**110%**
CLB LEVEL 2	**80%**
CLB LEVEL 3	**70%**
Goal for the session	**$90**
Estimated hands per hour	100
Maximum table limit	$500

Highest bet made in the entire series	**$57**
What hand did we make that bet?	90
What was the balance at that time?	$32

Highest balance achieved	**$184**
At what hand?	158

Lowest balance experienced	**($13)**
At what hand?	3

Goal amount achieved	**$94**
At what hand achieved?	**58**
Minutes required to achieve goal	34.8
Dollars wagered to reach the goal	$540
Total R.O.I. upon reaching goal	**17.41%**

Ending Series Balance	**$168**
Total dollars wagered in the entire series	$1,709
Total R.O.I. - the entire series	**9.83%**

No. of CLB-L1 bets to reach goal?	**2**
No. of CLB-L2 bets to reach goal?	0
No. of CLB-L3 bets to reach goal?	0

No. of CLB-L1 bets in the entire series?	**10**
No. of CLB-L2 bets in the entire series?	**3**
No. of CLB-L3 bets in the entire series?	0

43.13%	**WINS**	69
48.75%	**LOSSES**	78
8.13%	**PUSHES**	13
100.00%	**TOTAL**	**160**

FIGURE 10-3

Note that the highest bet you ever had to make was $57 at hand 90, which is really a very medium bet. The balance before you started the loss sequence that ended up in a win at hand 90, was $103; the ending balance after the win at the W5 CLB2 bet was $89, and you fully recovered to a balance of $105 at hand 98. Ain't life grand? If you scan the run in Figure 10-2, you'll see that you never had to make any really high bets throughout the entire series from start to finish. An important statistic also becomes evident here—in Chapter 9 the average number of CLB bets for an entire series was three; in this scenario we triple that amount. We made our goal of eighteen to twenty units on hand 58, or approximately thirty minutes of play. Consider this: If you were using $10 units, you would have made almost $200 in just around thirty minutes just going for the goal of eighteen to twenty units, and not even thinking about going the full eighty minutes of play!

Betting Models Suited to Each Type of 21 Game

What betting model is best suited for what type of 21 game? Realistically, your best bet for multideck play (shoes with four to eight decks) is a strategy that allows you to increment your bets upward slowly through the zone and into the various stages of CLB mode. The reason is this—you will hit longer losing streaks playing against multideck configurations. The strategy shown in Figure 10-1 is well suited for this kind of deck configuration and play. You could make this strategy even more conservative by making the CLB-1 bet 100% instead of 110%, or take the CLB-2 bets down to 70% from 80%. There are obviously all kinds of parameter changes you could make. Reciprocally, you could crank up these parameters to be more aggressive if you'd like.

If you prefer to play single- or double-deck configurations, as I do, you'll find that you'd lose five hands in row infrequently. The deck configuration is usually set at 50% penetration, leaving around fifty-two cards in play. If you play head-to-head against the dealer using an average of five to six cards per deal, you'll have around seven to eight deals before each shuffle. If you average only two to three wins per shuffle, the win/loss distribution may look something this:

Win-Lose-Lose-Lose-Win-Win-Lose-Lose
Shuffle
Lose-Lose-Win-Lose-Win-Win-Lose-Win
Shuffle
Win-Lose-Lose-Win-Lose-Lose-Win-Lose, and so on

I believe this is certainly what playing against a double or single deck looks like, with a single deck having a little more shuffling going on. Looking at this type of win/loss distribution, you can certainly design a betting system that is well suited for maximizing your potential. If you're a $5 bettor, your betting sequence would look something like the routine shown in Figure 10-4.

Pump up the bets a bit if you're confident you will achieve a win at least once out of five to seven hands of play. But never forget, get out and off the table once your goal is achieved. Let's analyze the statistics on this one.

We can see from this chart that you have indeed reached your goal at hand 41, or roughly twenty-four minutes of play. Note that the highest bet made was at hand 65 for the amount of $88, which is another medium to high bet; however, it occurred after you already made your goal. It pays to be aggressive at single or double deck because you're not often stretched to seven or even eight losses in a row. Even if you did go that far, you'd go into protection mode when leaving the zone, which always protects you from extended losses when they do occur, because you are, as you well know, at the unit minimum.

ADVANCED CLB STRATEGY - MODEL 5
Semi-Aggressive CLB-ZONE Stage Betting
(For a $5 Minimum Table and/or Base Unit size)

Tier Level Betting WIN Schema

Bet Code	Bet Amount	Double or Split OK	Chance of a Player Win	IF WIN GO TO	IF LOSS GO TO
THE ZONE					
W1	$5	Yes	12.500%	W2	L2
W2	$8	Yes	12.500%	W3	L2
W3	$5	Yes	9.375%	W4	L2
W4	$8	Yes	6.250%	W5	L2
W5	$5	Yes	3.906%	W4	L2
CLB STAGE 2					
W6	110-CLB	NO	12.500%	W1	L7
W7			BYPASSED		
W8	70-CLB	NO	12.500%	W8	L8
CLB STAGE 3 - OPTIONAL.					
W9	$8	Yes	12.500%	W10	L2
W10	$8	Yes	12.500%	W11	L2
W11	$5	Yes	9.375%	W1	L1

Tier Level Betting LOSS Schema

Bet Code	Bet Amount	Double or Split OK	Chance of a Dealer Win	WHEN WIN GO TO	IF LOSS GO TO
THE ZONE					
L1	$5	Yes	12.500%	W1	L2
L2	$10	Yes	12.500%	W1	L3
L3	$20	NO	9.375%	W1	L4
L4	110-CLB	NO	6.250%	W1	L5
L5	110-CLB	NO	3.906%	W1	L6
CLB STAGE 2					
L6	$5	Yes	Variable	W6	L6
L7	90-CLB	NO	Variable	W1	L8
L8	$5	Yes	Variable	W8	L8

FIGURE 10-4

SESSION STATISTICS

CLB LEVEL 1	**110%**
CLB LEVEL 2	**90%**
CLB LEVEL 3	**70%**
Goal for the session	**$90**
Estimated hands per hour	100
Maximum table limit	$500

Highest bet made in the entire series	**$88**
What hand did we make that bet?	65
What was the balance at that time?	$43

Highest balance achieved	**$166**
At what hand?	80

Lowest balance experienced	**($17)**
At what hand?	10

Goal amount achieved	**$95**
At what hand achieved?	**41**
Minutes required to achieve goal	24.6
Dollars wagered to reach the goal	$426
Total R.O.I. upon reaching goal	**22.30%**

Ending Series Balance	**$147**
Total dollars wagered in the entire series	$2,055
Total R.O.I. - the entire series	**7.15%**

No. of CLB-L1 bets to reach goal?	**1**
No. of CLB-L2 bets to reach goal?	0
No. of CLB-L3 bets to reach goal?	0

No. of CLB-L1 bets in the entire series?	**13**
No. of CLB-L2 bets in the entire series?	0
No. of CLB-L3 bets in the entire series?	0

43.13%	**WINS**	69
48.75%	**LOSSES**	78
8.13%	**PUSHES**	13
100.00%	**TOTAL**	**160**

FIGURE 10-5

Can You Change Strategies Midstream?

I'm often asked that question and it really answers itself. No one knows what's going to happen at the tables. For ten minutes you'll go through two to three shoes about even with the house, meaning it and you are winning hands evenly. Then all of a sudden you go from even, to the house starting to win 60% to 70% of the hands. Well, all you have to do is make a couple of small adjustments. Let's say you notice that the result distribution for the last couple of shoes looks something like this:

Lose-Lose-Lose-Lose-Lose-Win
Lose-Lose-Lose-Win
Lose-Lose-Lose-Win
Lose-Lose-Win
Lose-Lose-Lose-Lose-Win
Lose-Lose-Lose-Lose

So what do we have here? You win five out of twenty-six hands (about 19%), and the house wins the rest (81%). Of course your standard betting strategy already takes care of this slide, even going out to an L4 or even L5 bet. However, some of you may get a little nervous having to constantly extend yourself out four to five losing bets every time just to get one win, and I understand it can be a little aggravating. But don't get emotional, get smart! Watch what's happening with the cards! If you see this trend occurring on a consistent basis, then make adjustments. Every shoe gets its own personality for a few shuffles. The smart player recognizes the changes and adjusts accordingly. If I saw something like this situation occurring, I would probably extend my initial low dollar value bets an extra step or two to stop the base bets from getting so high that when I do go into stage 2 CLB, the recovery bets don't automatically get so high either. Please look at the adjusted strategy in Figure 10-6.

ADJUSTED STRATEGY - MODEL 6
Semi-Aggressive CLB-ZONE Stage Betting
(For a $5 Minimum Table and/or Base Unit size)

Tier Level Betting WIN Schema

Bet Code	Bet Amount	Double or Split OK	Chance of a Player Win	IF WIN GO TO	IF LOSS GO TO
THE ZONE					
W1	$5	Yes	12.500%	W2	L2
W2	$5	Yes	12.500%	W3	L2
W3	$5	Yes	9.375%	W4	L2
W4	$5	Yes	6.250%	W5	L2
W5	$5	Yes	3.906%	W4	L2
CLB STAGE 2					
W6	80-CLB	No	12.500%	W1	L7

Tier Level Betting LOSS Schema

Bet Code	Bet Amount	Double or Split OK	Chance of a Dealer Win	WHEN WIN GO TO	IF LOSS GO TO
THE ZONE					
L1	$5	Yes	12.500%	W1	L2
L2	$5	Yes	12.500%	W1	L3
L3	$5	No	9.375%	W1	L4
L4	$15	No	6.250%	W1	L5
L5	110-CLB	No	3.906%	W1	L6
CLB STAGE 2					
L6	90-CLB	Yes	Variable	W1	L7
L7	80-CLB	No	Variable	W1	L8
L8	$5	Yes	Variable	W6	L8

FIGURE 10-6

As you can see, you really lightened and extended your small bets on the initial losses right through bet L4 from $5 to $15 and kept all the win column bets at $5. Go for the total recapture of all losses plus profit on bet L5 with a 110%-CLB. If you still lose, than go for another 90%-CLB at bet L6. If you lose at L6, drop to L7 with an 80%-CLB, which ensures that if you do get a back-to-back win, you'll recapture most of the wagers right there. Now, if you lose again, drop into protection mode with a $5 bet, and keep betting at L8 until you see the win. Go to W6 for another 80%-CLB, and if you still don't win, go for a back-to-back 80%-CLB at L7, again looking for the back-to-back win. If there is still no win, go to L8 for protection mode again, and when you win, loop back to W6 and try that phase all over again. Of course, at any point that you experience a win, immediately go back to bet W1 and start a new sequence. This entire process is better understood with a chart that runs out a series of seventy-five bets, so here we have one in Figure 10-7.

The object of this betting strategy is, of course, to withstand an inordinate amount of losses and still stay in the hunt with a bankroll that doesn't get too badly demolished. The series of losses we just discussed demonstrates how the CLB methodology can really save your hide when the cards go sour. Let's look at the statistics on this short run of losses in Figure 10-8.

Notice that you never met your goal, but is that bad? In this case, you need to be thankful that you exited this bloody battlefield with your life and bankroll still intact! As Figure 10-8 shows, you suffered more than 2:1 in losses versus wins and still ended up showing a marginal profit (see the wins, losses, and pushes percentages at the bottom of the figure). Do you think maybe there's something to this CLB stuff? You bet there is! And for an added bonus, you never had to make a bet higher than $57 at hand 6, which is just a medium recovery bet.

FIGURE 10-7

RANDOM RUN FOR (75) RESULTS — $5 BET UNITS — MODEL 6

HAND NO.	BET CODE	BET AMT	RESULT	GAIN/ LOSS	RUNNING BALANCE	CLB ACCRUAL
INITIAL	W1	$5	L	($5)	($5)	($5)
2	L2	$5	L	($5)	($10)	($10)
3	L3	$5	L	($5)	($15)	($15)
4	L4	$15	L	($15)	($30)	($30)
5	L5 CLB1	$33	L	($33)	($63)	($63)
6	L6 CLB2	$57	WIN	$57	($6)	$0
7	W1	$5	L	($5)	($11)	($5)
8	L2	$5	WIN	$5	($6)	$0
9	W1	$5	L	($5)	($11)	($5)
10	L2	$5	WIN	$5	($6)	$0
11	W1	$5	WIN	$5	($1)	$0
12	W2	$5	L	($5)	($6)	($5)
13	L2	$5	L	($5)	($11)	($10)
14	L3	$5	L	($5)	($16)	($15)
15	L4	$15	L	($15)	($31)	($30)
16	L5 CLB1	$33	WIN	$33	$2	$0
17	W1	$5	L	($5)	($3)	($5)
18	L2	$5	L	($5)	($8)	($10)
19	L3	$5	WIN	$5	($3)	$0
20	W1	$5	L	($5)	($8)	($5)
21	L2	$5	L	($5)	($13)	($10)
22	L3	$5	L	($5)	($18)	($15)
23	L4	$15	WIN	$15	($3)	$0
24	W1	$5	L	($5)	($8)	($5)
25	L2	$5	L	($5)	($13)	($10)
26	L3	$5	L	($5)	($18)	($15)
27	L4	$15	L	($15)	($33)	($30)
28	L5 CLB1	$33	WIN	$33	$0	$0
29	W1	$5	L	($5)	($5)	($5)
30	L2	$5	L	($5)	($10)	($10)
31	L3	$5	L	($5)	($15)	($15)
32	L4	$15	L	($15)	($30)	($30)

HAND NO.	BET CODE	BET AMT	RESULT	GAIN/ LOSS	RUNNING BALANCE	CLB ACCRUAL
33	L5 CLB1	$33	PUSH	$0	($30)	($30)
34	L5	$33	PUSH	$0	($30)	($30)
35	L5	$33	WIN	$33	$3	$0
36	W1	$5	WIN	$5	$8	$0
37	W2	$5	L	($5)	$3	($5)
38	L2	$5	L	($5)	($2)	($10)
39	L3	$5	L	($5)	($7)	($15)
40	L4	$15	L	($15)	($22)	($30)
41	L5 CLB1	$33	WIN	$33	$11	$0
42	W1	$5	PUSH	$0	$11	$0
43	W1	$5	WIN	$5	$16	$0
44	W2	$5	L	($5)	$11	($5)
45	L2	$5	L	($5)	$6	($10)
46	L3	$5	L	($5)	$1	($15)
47	L4	$15	WIN	$15	$16	$0
48	W1	$5	L	($5)	$11	($5)
49	L2	$5	WIN	$5	$16	$0
50	W1	$5	PUSH	$0	$16	$0
51	W1	$5	L	($5)	$11	($5)
52	L2	$5	L	($5)	$6	($10)
53	L3	$5	L	($5)	$1	($15)
54	L4	$15	WIN	$15	$16	$0
55	W1	$5	L	($5)	$11	($5)
56	L2	$5	L	($5)	$6	($10)
57	L3	$5	WIN	$5	$11	$0
58	W1	$5	WIN	$5	$16	$0
59	W2	$5	PUSH	$0	$16	$0
60	W2	$5	WIN	$5	$21	$0
61	W3	$5	L	($5)	$16	($5)
62	L2	$5	L	($5)	$11	($10)
63	L3	$5	L	($5)	$6	($15)
64	L4	$15	L	($15)	($9)	($30)
65	L5 CLB1	$33	WIN	$33	$24	$0
66	W1	$5	L	($5)	$19	($5)

HAND NO.	BET CODE	BET AMT	RESULT	GAIN/ LOSS	RUNNING BALANCE	CLB ACCRUAL
67	L2	$5	L	($5)	$14	($10)
68	L3	$5	L	($5)	$9	($15)
69	L4	$15	WIN	$15	$24	$0
70	W1	$5	L	($5)	$19	($5)
71	L2	$5	WIN	$5	$24	$0
72	W1	$5	L	($5)	$19	($5)
73	L2	$5	PUSH	$0	$19	($5)
74	L2	$5	WIN	$5	$24	$0
75	W1	$5	PUSH	$0	$24	$0

Of course, I certainly do not recommend that you stay seventy-five hands and endure something like this. Once you recognize you're losing more than winning, then you can use this strategy to either get even quickly, or minimize your losses until you decide to get out. In the session analyzed in Figure 10-8, I would have recognized this condition by around hand 25, quit, and been satisfied with the $13 loss. No, I'm not clairvoyant, but I've played enough shoes to know when it's better just to save myself the aggravation and find another table that offers a better win ratio opportunity. This example clearly shows what I've said in earlier chapters—see what a shoe is doing before sitting down, and you'll save yourself a lot of aggravation. If you're looking for a head-to-head game, then this is a moot point. But if you happen to see just one person at the table and things look good, by all means take a seat and give it a try!

SESSION STATISTICS

CLB LEVEL 1	**110%**
CLB LEVEL 2	**90%**
CLB LEVEL 3	**80%**
Goal for the session	**$90**
Estimated hands per hour	100
Maximum table limit	$500

Highest bet made in the entire series	**$57**
What hand did we make that bet?	6
What was the balance at that time?	($63)

Highest balance achieved	**$24**
At what hand?	65

Lowest balance experienced	**($63)**
At what hand?	5

Goal amount achieved	**NA**
At what hand achieved?	NA
Minutes required to achieve goal	NA
Dollars wagered to reach the goal	NA
Total R.O.I. upon reaching goal	**NA**

Ending Series Balance	**$24**
Total dollars wagered in the entire series	$751
Total R.O.I. - the entire series	**3.20%**

No. of CLB-L1 bets to reach goal?	**NA**
No. of CLB-L2 bets to reach goal?	NA
No. of CLB-L3 bets to reach goal?	NA

No. of CLB-L1 bets in the entire series?	**6**
No. of CLB-L2 bets in the entire series?	**1**
No. of CLB-L3 bets in the entire series?	0

43.13%	**WINS**	22
48.75%	**LOSSES**	46
8.13%	**PUSHES**	7
100.00%	**TOTAL**	**75**

FIGURE 10-8

The Takedown Strategy

Blackjack has been around for so long, and so many supposed "systems" have been developed to enable folks to overcome the game. Many of the systems are viable. I, myself, look upon my CLB method as more of a strategy than a system. A system implies that one has discovered a solution to the problem that will work every time, whereas a strategy is more of a tactical method geared toward problem resolution for a given situation but is not a guarantee of resolution. In my opinion, the best anyone can do is stick with whatever strategy he or she would like to use and not deviate from it. Make adjustments when necessary, but stick with the mainstream method as your play ensues. For example, let's say you have a doubling hand that needs a high card and you're counting high cards; two players ahead of you hit their hands with high cards. If the strategy you're using allows you to double, then maybe you shouldn't this time and just hit. Making on-the-fly adjustments and paying attention can really save you in these situations.

A popular method used by many folks capitalizes on subsequent or repeated wins, and keeps losses at the unit minimum. It's called by many names, but most folks I know call it the "profit takedown" or "takedown" method. The strategy is shown in Figure 10-9.

As you can see, you increase your bet by 50% for each win achieved while "taking down" 50% of your profit. You do it three times in a row, and then regress to the original bet. At any point you lose, you just stay at $10 until a win is achieved; then you go back to bet W1. It's just that simple. Please keep in mind that this strategy works best when you're getting a better than even distribution of winning hands, but it will carve you up if the cards start favoring the house, because there's no recovery component to this strategy other than just betting the unit minimum. Therefore, if you were to step up and bet bigger after each of the two wins and then lose three to four in a row, you would slowly dig yourself a

PROFIT TAKEDOWN STRATEGY - MODEL 7
Moderate Betting Strategy
(For a $10 Minimum Table and/or Base Unit size)

Tier Level Betting WIN Schema

Bet Code	Bet Amount	Double or Split OK	Chance of a Player Win	IF WIN GO TO	IF LOSS GO TO
		THE ZONE			
W1	$10	Yes	12.500%	W2	L1
W2	$15	Yes	12.500%	W3	L1
W3	$20	No	9.375%	W4	L1
W4	$10	No	6.250%	W5	L1
W5	$15	No	3.906%	W6	L1
W6	$20	No	2.344%	W1	L1

Tier Level Betting LOSS Schema

Bet Code	Bet Amount	Double or Split OK	Chance of a Dealer Win	WHEN WIN GO TO	IF LOSS GO TO
		THE ZONE			
L1	$10	Yes	12.500%	W2	L2
L2	$10	Yes	12.500%	W2	L3
L3	$10	No	9.375%	W2	L4
L4	$10	No	6.250%	W2	L5
L5	$10	No	3.906%	W2	L6
L6	$10	No	2.344%	W2	L1

FIGURE 10-9

nice money hole that would just keep getting deeper and deeper and you'd never climb out of it!

You can clearly see why this strategy remains a favorite with many of the professionals out there because you increase your bet only while you are winning, and decrease to the table minimum when you are losing. In my opinion this is just fine so long as the cards are favoring the player, but of course this is usually not the case, but the exception.

The essence of this strategy is to begin pulling back any of your profits during the winning series. It's important to understand the probabilities laid out in Figure 10-9, because you aren't going to win indefinitely. At some point during the winning series you have to bring some of your profits in and make lower bets. It's just that plain and simple. You can adjust this strategy any way that you want; you can stretch out the win sequence one more bet, or you can even couple up some losing exponents on the loss side instead of just betting the base unit of $10 after each consecutive loss. It's your choice, of course.

But one thing is very true in gambling and specifically the casino industry, and that is this: The house fears only one thing—a player who isn't afraid to fully press or partially press his bets as he is winning. What does "press" the bet mean? Take all the winnings and let it ride possibly two to three times in a row. A $50 to $100 bettor can really hurt a smaller casino by getting several winning series in a row. If the player's hands are getting hot, meaning the player is winning four out of five hands consistently, this is a way to go. It might look something like this for a $25 bettor partially pressing the base bet of $25 out two to three more hands and then pulling back to the base bet of $25 again (BBB means "back to base bet"):

Win(25)-Win(38)-Win(57)-{BBB}
Win25(WinDblDn25)-Win(38)-Lose(57)-{BBB}
Win(25)-Lose(38)-Win(25)-Win(38)-Win(57)(WinSplit57)-{BBB}
Win(25)-Win(38)-Win(57)(WinDblDn57)-{BBB}

Lose(25)-Lose(25)-Win(25)-Win(38)(WinDblDn38)-
Win(57)-{BBB}
Win(25)-Win(38)-Lose(57)-{BBB}
Win(25)-Win(38)-Win(57)

So how does this play translate into dollars? About $726 in about ten minutes or twenty-five hands of play, and that's not bad. Notice that pressing of the bets extended out to only three wins, including double downs and splits, and then the sequence started over again. If you were using $100 units, you would have been up around $2,900 or so. This is a very substantial win in the game of 21 because, the game of 21 is considered a pretty even game—house against the player with only a slight edge going to the house. This method is very effective when a streak is in progress, but will kill you if the win/loss sequence begins to chop like this:

Win(25)-Lose(50)-Win(25)-Lose(50)

You get the idea. Every time you win and press the bet to $50 you lose, meaning you are losing every other hand and going negative $25. It happens, and when it does, you need to change up the table really fast by adding a second hand, possibly reduce a hand if you are playing two, wait for another player to join you, or just leave the table! Pay attention to what you're doing and what's happening, adjust your betting strategy on the fly if you have to, but just don't let yourself get hammered and do nothing like most folks do! Use this method when you want to be conservative yet maximize a short set of wins and hedge your bets by increasing them slightly yet taking profits back in a limited way.

All in all, when using this method you should always end up in a profit situation after a small series of wins. A note of caution: Typically where strategy tells you to double down, just take the hit instead. Because if you double or split and lose, you may jeopardize the additional winnings you've accumulated during the series and get wiped out! Believe it or not, some folks who get on a winning streak believe that they're invincible and just end up burying themselves after all is said and done.

I have another story to illustrate this scenario. Not too long ago, I went into a local casino that offered a double-deck game with average rules—doubling allowed only on 9-10-11 and the dealer hits soft 17. I met up with an old acquaintance who was at the table, and he looked like he was doing okay. He had about $160 in chips, and as I watched, he was using the strategy depicted in Figure 10-9. He was kicking the house's behind! He was certainly winning an average of seven out of ten hands, and they were dispersed perfectly so that when he lost a hand he would lose two in a row at the bet minimum, and when he started winning he'd win three to five hands in a row. He was even doubling and splitting to the third winning bet (which, if you recall, I don't recommend) and was even winning those! I asked him what his buy-in was and he said it was $80 (again, I don't recommend even start-ing without the 40(x) session money) and that he's never looked back from bet number one! He said, "I'm using the takedown, and I'm kicking 'em sideways and front ways!" I was very excited for him! I stayed and watched for about forty minutes while he clobbered the house. During that time, he had taken his original $80 to about $1,250. Wow! He literally killed the house with a minimum bankroll, and trust me, that very rarely happens!

You might be waiting for an "I told you so" ending, but there actually isn't one. The composition of the cards always goes south, and for him it did as well; however, he realized the change in a small series of losses, losing only around $75, and he knew the party was over! This is a classic success story because he was paying attention to the composition of the shoe (double deck in that casino is dealt from a shoe), mak-ing the necessary adjustments along the way with a final pull-out when the composition totally changed. This act alone allows me to pay him the highest accolade of all—he exuded total control and discipline, kept his head, knew the odds, and got the heck out with the casino's money!

Having said that, I've also witnessed many folks using this method making 200% to 300% of their buy-in money in quick time, then hitting a streak of losses, and watching everything they just made get wiped out. This reinforces my statement that when you reach a goal, place the profits in lock-up mode and continue adding to the lock-up money as you are winning, but never use it to cover bets when you start losing. This ensures victory each and every time!

Winning Consistently

By now you must be thinking, "How can I ensure that I will win consistently using the methods presented thus far?" The entire purpose of these pages is to assist you in playing the game without counting cards. It is my firm belief that you can win most of the time using these methods, especially the CLB methods, because I win most times that I go out to play! I actually win more now than I ever did counting the cards! You can also hedge your strategies by employing some casual counting during the game. This will be explained in Chapter 12. So, whether you casual count, use true card-counting methods, or not, never forget that the probabilities of winning and losing consecutive hands still exist, and the zone still exists.

The key is to understand the advanced strategies discussed in this chapter and tailor one that fits your needs and threshold of nervous tension. Remember, this is gambling in the strictest sense—there are no guarantees, although I wish I could say that there were! The best security a gambler can ever hope for comes from good discipline, knowing the odds, using some sort of playing and betting methods, understanding that winning most times comes slowly, and just to stick with it. Setting your goal for the session's win is probably the most critical decision you must make, again, *before* you enter the casino!

WHAT IS THE HOUSE EDGE?

Most folks in the gaming industry say the house edge is about .2% to 1% in the house's favor (all possible rules and variations), which is probably close. So what does that mean? Technically it means that for every 100 hands dealt, over the long haul, the house will win about 51% of the hands, discounting pushes. That may not seem like much, but it's a lot when you are wagering $10 hands at the rate of eighty hands per hour, not counting doubles and splits. That equates to about 800 bucks an hour! And 1% is the edge if you are playing perfect basic strategy with no mistakes. The percentage goes way up if you're not playing correctly. You may as well just mail your money in and skip the trip, and that's no joke!

Turning the Tables on the House's Edge

Turning the tables on the house's edge is what all playing and betting strategies are about. Ensuring that you, the player, make that extra dough for every hundred bucks wagered, instead of giving it to the house is what is *key*. Can it be done?

You bet! It's done by thousands of folks every day of the year. Can you make a living doing it? Absolutely. But would you want to? Probably not because it's a tough way to make a living, although the working hours are great! Let's say you need to make $400 a day to live. You'd have to bet at least $25 to $50 per hand and get ten to twenty chips ahead in any given day. So you think, gee, that doesn't sound too tough; I could do that pretty easily. Wrong! Did I forget to mention that sometimes you'll need to bet possibly $250 to go with some of the strategies we've discussed in earlier chapters, especially CLB strategy Model-1 in Figure 9-2? It puts a lump in your throat, doesn't it? Exposing your bankroll to the house is always very dangerous. The element of risk is astounding!

Making a living playing 21 has other shortcomings, too. The tension of having to make a profit daily is a tremendous drain on your brain. Trust me, I've been there. So is having to put up with folks who get mad because they lost everything, or with drunks from time to time, or strangers wanting to borrow money. (Can you believe that? Strangers, no less. The nerve of those folks!) Then there are the dealers who are less than cordial, pit bosses who love to see you suffer or distract you (never me, that's for sure; I never give them the pleasure), and people who get so excited they spill their drinks all over you or the layout on the table. These are just to name a few. But I digress—I was telling you about the house's edge.

Another way to look at the house's edge, as exaggerated as I may make it seem, is in a combination of factors: the average rule variants in all the casinos, understanding the basics of the game (playing strategy), betting strategy, and discipline and patience. *Here is my computation.* Most folks don't know how to play the game correctly (folks who just plain *don't understand the basics of game* before sitting down—just in it for the fun, with no playing strategy whatsoever!). This bumps up the house's edge, in my book, to an off-the-cuff 5%. *Betting with no strategy* in mind bumps it up another estimated 5%— money management is one of the cornerstones of gambling!

Using the original .5% (which is based on combining all the possible deck configurations, rules, and bet limitations; it's a rule of thumb used by most professionals in the industry), we can begin adding things up. No understanding of the game (no playing strategy) equals −5%, no betting strategy equals −5%, and rule variants between types of games offered equals −.5% . . . I guess that's about −10.5% stacked against those folks. You can clearly see how heavy I weight just under-standing the game coupled with money management. These are the two factors that can really be anyone's downfall! Now combine all that with another estimated −5% for using no dis-cipline or patience while at the table (meaning no goal setting, not leaving a table when things turn sour, etc.)—players would be lucky to get out with their shirts still on at −15.5%!

This may sound like a radical way of describing the house's edge, and surely I've made some applied mathematicians and actuaries roll over and scream, but quite simply, the house's "big edge" is that it can outlast you, me, and everybody else. It doesn't matter what the computed edge is so much as the sta-tistics and behavior of the people who play the games! Most folks can't overcome the biggest obstacle in gaming –them-selves! Casinos are nothing but patient because they're not going anywhere. They're just waiting for greed, stupidity, and impatience to kick in, and for their patrons to dump off their money, which nearly 99% of their patrons will do! Now you know why those casinos in Las Vegas and everywhere else have so many blackjack tables and keep getting fancier as each year passes. At those odds I'd love to build and own one myself. That's where the real cheesecake is, baby!

Stick to Your Strategy, Control Your Emotions, and Beat the Odds!

There are professionals who will dispute the way I calculate the house edge, but I've been playing this game for more than twenty-five years and have seen many folks buy in to a table for a hundred bucks, last about thirty to sixty minutes, and poof, their money vaporizes. If that isn't a house edge computed the way I just did it, I don't know what is! That's why it is imperative for you to utilize a playing and betting strategy that you feel comfortable with, whether outlined within these pages or developed on your own. You stand a much better chance of being successful by being consistent.

It is also why I place such heavy emphasis on discipline and patience. Here we are analyzing the game for effective playing and betting strategies, but you can see the human, or rather the emotional component, is equally, if not *more* important than all the rest. It's a cliché, but if you have all the tools and fix the problem (achieve your goal), but still keep tinkering (stay at the table), something else is bound to break (you'll begin taking losses), and it usually does.

At the risk of being repetitive, patience employed in this game is pure gold and your greatest asset! When things are going badly—being dealt eight stiffs in a row (a two-card total between 12 and 16 with the dealer having a seven or greater showing)—your only friend is patience because, as surely as those cards went against you, great cards will generally balance out the shoe within a few shuffles. Making the right decisions when cards fall badly for you separates the men from the boys. The game of blackjack is a very *tough* and *long* grind most of the time.

So maybe you're asking yourself, "What is the toughest thing I'll have to deal with?" The answer is having enough discipline to leave when you've accumulated your eighteen-unit profit goal! If you are playing for $3 or $5 units, eighteen units doesn't sound like much; for $3 units it's $54 and for $5 units it's $90. But listen, it took you only about sixty to eighty minutes in a maximum time frame to do it, maybe in even less time, and that's not bad.

Here comes the exciting news. If you can exercise all the playing, betting, and emotional components we've discussed thus far, you may be able to consistently attain decent profit

PROFIT AND EARN RATE ANALYSIS				
UNIT AMOUNT	BUY-IN AMOUNT	18-UNIT PROFIT	ENDING SESSION AMT	WIN RATE PER HOUR
$3	$120	$54	$174	$46
$5	$200	$90	$290	$77
$10	$400	$180	$580	$154
$15	$600	$270	$870	$231
$25	$1,000	$450	$1,450	$386
$50	$2,000	$900	$2,900	$771
$75	$3,000	$1,350	$4,350	$1,157
$100	$4,000	$1,800	$5,800	$1,543
$250	$10,000	$4,500	$14,500	$3,857
$500	$20,000	$9,000	$29,000	$7,714
$1,000	$40,000	$18,000	$58,000	$15,429
BAIL-OUT POINTS IN ORDER OF PRIORITY				
[1] Eighteen-unit profit goal attained or 60–80 minutes of session play, whichever is first.				
[2] Session money reaches 15%–20% or below of original session buy-in.				

FIGURE 11-1

rates. Figure 11-1 shows what the eighteen-unit profit is equivalent to for the different unit bets, and what the win rate per hour could look like for you:

As you view this figure it may or may not look realistic to you. But I'm here to tell you that the numbers can be achieved on a regular basis if you are committed to reaching the eighteen-unit goal and sticking with it, meaning that once you reach your goal, you're prepared to either take a break, then find another table, or leave satisfied with the day's profits. Remember, it's okay to bail out after making only ten units or so; nobody is going to think less of you and you shouldn't think less of yourself. If for some reason you get an overwhelming feeling of impending doom, anxiety (butterflies), or any negative feelings at all, just take a break. It's better to leave with a little than nothing at all.

Leaving While Winning

I often hear from folks who say, "Hey, if I'm winning, why should I leave?" And that's a good question! There's a way to accomplish both desires. Let's assume you're at a seventeen-unit profit level, you just doubled down and won your bet, and now you're at a twenty-one-unit profit level. Who knows, you may be on a winning streak, especially if you won the last two deals. So here's what you do. Set aside the eighteen units and play with the three extra units you have left. If you keep winning, after each win set aside two more units, one in your eighteen-unit stack, and one in your current playing stake. The minute you lose 50% of the additional units you've set aside in your current playing stake, *stop!* You're finished with this session. It's as easy as that. You've satisfied your desire to see the winning streak out and you've exerted great discipline in setting aside your original eighteen-unit profit goal and not placing it in jeopardy, plus now you have additional units beyond your original win goal. At this point you should be very happy with yourself and ready to do it again— after an extended break, of course!

WHAT IS THE 46% RULE
AND THE CASUAL COUNT?

ere's a revelation that is not so obvious to most folks. Did you realize that 46% of the cards in the deck are high-value cards? It's true. Check this out: nine, ten, jack, queen, king, ace. You know there are fifty-two cards in a deck; therefore, six high cards times four suits equals twenty-four cards, right? Twenty-four is 46% of fifty-two. By that simplistic analysis you can determine your play and betting by watching cards coming out as they're dealt. Let's see how that works. Assume you're at a double-deck game with one other player at the table, and so far the hands look like this:

	Status	Action	Card	Action	Card	Action
Player 1	K, 3					
Player 2	2, 7					
Dealer Up Card	8, ?					

So, what are you looking at here? Five cards have been shown, and only 20% of them are classified as high value.

What do you do? Because it's a fresh shuffle, it's still hard to tell with so few cards out, but this should be the play:

	Status	Action	Card	Action	Card	Action
Player 1	K, 3	Hits	5	Stand		
Player 2	2, 7	Hits	7	Hits	6	Busts
Dealer Up						
Card	8, ?	Flips	Q	Stands		

So, let's analyze what we have here. Two of our nine cards shown are high-value cards, which equal around 22% high cards shown thus far. What do you bet that the next sequence gets more higher cards than lower cards? Let's see on the next deal:

	Status	Action	Card	Action	Card	Action
Player 1	9, A	Stands				
Player 2	3, 3	Splits				
Dealer Up						
Card	6, ?					

What do we have here to analyze before decision time? So far, four out of our fourteen cards shown are high-value cards, or 28%, still well below the 46% average of what it should be. How does this information help you? You haven't seen the dealer's "hole" card (the card the dealer has under his visible card), so what do you think are the chances the dealer has a ten-value card under there? Pretty high, right? So, what does Player 2 need to do? She realizes that there haven't been too many ten-value cards coming out, so does it make sense to split the threes? Even though the strategy cards say to do it, why would you? It's likely that Player 2 would split to two ten-value cards and have two 13s against the dealer's 6; not bad, but why take the chance? Why not just hit the 3s, and let the dealer break his potential 16? Here's what happens:

	Status	Action	Card	Action	Card	Action
Player 1	9, A	Stands				
Player 2	3, 3	Hits	10	Stands		
Dealer Up						
Card	6	Flips	Q	Hits	8	Busts

What you've just witnessed is called *casual counting*—looking casually at the cards coming out, but not assigning point values as you would in regular card counting. All you have to do is count the nines, tens, and aces versus all the cards that you've seen. In the preceding examples, after all the hands have been played, we have some serious information about the cards left in the shoe or in the dealer's hand. The final tally is six out of sixteen cards, or roughly 38%, have been high-value cards. As you can see, having this information is helpful in doubling and splitting hands against whatever the dealer may be showing, and estimating what his "hole" may be if the count is really low, meaning there have been fewer high cards seen than low cards. Note that if the percentage is low, you know the chances are high that higher cards will appear in the next sequence; therefore, you can adjust your betting accordingly because the chance of getting 19s, 20s, and 21s is very high—and that, my friends, is why we casual count. In casual counting, there's no brain strain, no fatigue factor; it's just a simple way of tracking the high cards as they are dealt, getting the information on what the composition of the unseen cards are, and going from there.

By the way, it is easier to casual count with more players at the table than going head-to-head against the dealer. Generally when you go head-to-head, the cards are dealt so quickly that you're forced to make playing decisions quickly, and that's tough enough, let alone trying to casually count the high cards at the same time. If you are going head-to-head against the dealer, the deal should be pretty even in winning hands: therefore, using the CLB betting strategy makes sense because it's difficult to lose more than three to five hands in a row going head-to-head against the dealer.

Casual counting gives you, the player, an exceptional advantage, especially when making decisions on double downs, splitting pairs, and taking insurance against the dealer's ace. If you have a friend with you at the table, he or she can count the high cards while you count all the cards that come out. Then all you have to do is make the simple division to obtain the ratio, and voilà—you have information! Or, if you're playing alone, when buying in for chips ask for dollar chips, about thirty to forty of them, and create little stacks in front of your session money to assist you in tracking either the number of high cards you see, or all the other cards, or even both. You can use this same method in tracking the number of wins and losses in any given series as well.

A Few Words on Spanish 21

There are a few variations on the game of 21: progressive blackjack, multiaction blackjack, double-exposure blackjack, and, my favorite, Spanish 21. This game is different from the others because the number ten cards are removed and the face cards remain. Obviously, removing the tens gives the house a slight advantage in odds over the standard game of 21. But the house more than makes up for that by giving the players some really great bonus options and plays that, when properly leveraged, give the advantage to the players. Here are some of the bonus options and plays you'll find in Spanish 21:

- A player's natural 21 always wins immediately and pays 3:2.
- A player's three-or-more 21 always beats the dealer's 21 and pays even money.
- A player can double down after more than two cards (a gigantic advantage!).
- A player can surrender half his or her bet after doubling down if the double is unfavorable, which is known as "double-down rescue."

- A player can hit and double down after splitting aces.
- A player can late surrender his or her initial two cards dealt after checking for blackjacks.
- A five-card 21 pays 3:2, a six-card 21 pays 2:1, and a seven-card 21 pays 3:1.
- A hand of 6-7-8 or 7-7-7 of mixed suits pays 3:2, a 6-7-8 or 7-7-7 of the same suit pays 2:1, and if made in spades it pays 3:1.
- A suited 7-7-7 that matches the dealer's up card pays $1,000 for bets between $5 and $24, and $5,000 for bets of $25 and over. At some casinos the other players at the table also receive a $50 bonus in the event of a $5,000 payoff. This bonus rule doesn't apply if the sevens are reached as a result of splitting.
- All 21 special bonus hands do not apply if they are the result of doubling down.
- Most casinos that have this game usually hit soft 17s.
- Some casinos allow the splitting of unmatched face cards, such as a jack with a queen, and so on.
- Most casinos use six decks from the shoe in dealing this game (less the tens, of course). This option varies in Las Vegas, Reno, Tahoe, Atlantic City, and most of the tribal casinos. Some of the Atlantic City casinos use an eight-deck shoe, but, again, it varies.
- Some casinos also have an additional side bet on the layout called "Match Play." Should the player option to make this bet, she hopes that one or both of her initial cards match the dealer's up card. If either one or both of the cards match the dealer's, the player is paid 4:1 on each unsuited match and 9:1 on suited matches. This option is very popular, but be warned: The house's edge on this option is almost 6%. Therefore, it isn't a great bet unless you're playing the odds and waiting for a long series of nonmatching hands and then begin using a moderate negative progression scheme. See Figures 14-1 and 14-2 for further information.

So What's So Great about Spanish 21?

If you've been paying attention, you now realize that the composition of the shoe is getting much different. Let's analyze:

2-3-4-5-6-7-8-9	Eight cards are low or neutral
A-K-Q-J	Four cards are high

Gee whiz, there are more low cards than high cards by almost a 2:1 ratio? Hmmm? Most blackjack experts will tell you that this is a tremendous advantage for the house. I can tell you that maybe mathematically it is, but the house now has to draw to those low cards, too, and it can't surrender, it can't double down on more than two cards, and when it gets twenty-one it's no big deal because there's *no* bonus for the house! Players definitely shouldn't insure against any dealer's ace (why would you? there are twice as many low cards than in a standard blackjack game), and many players double down on hard 12s and 13s, and make them. I see it happen all the time. I'll sometimes double on a hard 12 against the dealer's 5, 6, or even 7! The splitting and doubling combo becomes a terrific edge for players because they are apt to make more pat hands (hands totaling between 17 and 21), since there more low cards composing the shoe. The double-down rescue (surrender after doubling) option is great as well, in the event that the player doubles and gets a low card! I'll take the option of getting half my bet back any day of the year when I get a weak hand— and you should too! Always double-down rescue whenever you receive a doubled total of 12 through 16 against the dealer's eight through ace, or your 17 against the dealer's ace.

Here's a special insight into Spanish 21 from the casino bosses themselves! On my last trip to Las Vegas, I was hard-pressed to find any Spanish 21 tables at the larger casinos. My friend and I asked a couple of the bosses at some of the more noteworthy casinos, and they all said the casinos took the games out because the nightly hold (the house's profit) on

Spanish 21 wasn't as good as it is for the regular 21 games. Okay reader, that should tell you something right there. Casinos put games in that make them money, and, as I suspected, even with those tens missing, the edge in Spanish 21 really goes to the experienced player who knows how to leverage the options offered in this game. As far as I'm concerned, if you have access to playing Spanish 21, by all means give those casinos all your action; you won't be sorry that you did! An additional note: the house's edge on this game is just marginally more than a standard game of six-deck blackjack (.5%) where the dealer stands on soft 17; in Spanish 21 where the dealer hits soft 17, the house's edge is .8%.

What Is the Playing Strategy for Spanish 21?

Remember, even though this game offers many more options and bonuses, you still should casually count the cards as they come out. The even-up percentage is 33%, so it's only to your advantage to count. I recommend highly that you sit at either first base (the first seat at the table) or third base (the last seat at the table) while playing Spanish 21.

When you look at Figure 13-1, you'll see some playing strategies that may seem very unorthodox from the standard 21 game, but remember, there are twice as many low cards as high ones in this game. That's why you'd hit a player's 12 against the dealer's up card of five, and so on. The strategies in Figure 13-1 are mathematically correct, with millions of hands played. Figure 13-2 depicts the strategies I use most often in this game, after having played and watched thousands of hands. Again, some of the strategies may seem very unorthodox, but they have worked for me! Remember, you're not sitting down to play millions of hands; you're sitting down for a couple of hundred hands, so adjust your strategy as you play and watch the trends in the game. Again, what is "theoretically" correct play is presumed correct over a large sample of simulated hands played. What I try to do is give you the

SPANISH 21 SIX-DECK BLACKJACK

DEALER HITS A SOFT 17

HARD HAND STRATEGY

VALUE OF THE DEALER'S UP CARD

YOUR HAND	2	3	4	5	6	7	8	9	10	Ace
9	H	H	H	H	DD	H	H	H	H	H
10	DD	DD	DD	DD	DD	DD	DD	H	H	H
11	DD	DD	DD	DD	DD	DD	DD	DD	DD	DD
12	H	H	H	H	H	H	H	H	H	H
13	H	H	H	H	S	H	H	H	H	H
14	H	H	S	S	S	H	H	H	H	H
15	S	S	S	S	S	H	H	H	H	H
16	S	S	S	S	S	H	H	H	H	SR
17	S	S	S	S	S	S	S	S	S	SR

SOFT HAND STRATEGY

VALUE OF THE DEALER'S UP CARD

YOUR HAND	2	3	4	5	6	7	8	9	10	Ace
Ace, 2	H	H	H	H	H	H	H	H	H	H
Ace, 3	H	H	H	H	H	H	H	H	H	H
Ace, 4	H	H	H	H	DD	H	H	H	H	H
Ace, 5	H	H	H	DD	DD	H	H	H	H	H
Ace, 6	H	H	DD	DD	DD	H	H	H	H	H
Ace, 7	S	S	DD	DD	DD	S	S	H	H	H
Ace, 8	S	S	S	S	S	S	S	S	S	S
Ace, 9	S	S	S	S	S	S	S	S	S	S

PAIR SPLITTING STRATEGY

VALUE OF THE DEALER'S UP CARD

YOUR HAND	2	3	4	5	6	7	8	9	10	Ace
2 - 2	SPLIT	SPLIT	SPLIT	SPLIT	SPLIT	SPLIT	H	H	H	H
3 - 3	SPLIT	SPLIT	SPLIT	SPLIT	SPLIT	SPLIT	SPLIT	H	H	H
4 - 4	H	H	H	H	H	H	H	H	II	H
5 - 5	DD	DD	DD	DD	DD	DD	DD	H	H	H
6 - 6	H	H	SPLIT	SPLIT	SPLIT	H	H	H	H	H
7 - 7	SPLIT	SPLIT	SPLIT	SPLIT	SPLIT	SPLIT	H	H	H	H
8 - 8	SPLIT	SPLIT	SPLIT	SPLIT	SPLIT	SPLIT	SPLIT	SPLIT	SPLIT	SR
9 - 9	S	SPLIT	SPLIT	SPLIT	SPLIT	S	SPLIT	SPLIT	S	S
10 - 10	S	S	S	S	S	S	S	S	S	S
ACE, ACE	SPLIT	SPLIT	SPLIT	SPLIT	SPLIT	SPLIT	SPLIT	SPLIT	SPLIT	SPLIT

LEGEND

HIT	H
STAND	S
DOUBLE DOWN	DD
SPLIT THE PAIR	SPLIT
SURRENDER	SR

FIGURE 13-1

MODIFIED SPANISH 21 STRATEGY
DEALER HITS A SOFT 17

HARD HAND STRATEGY

VALUE OF THE DEALER'S UP CARD

YOUR HAND	2	3	4	5	6	7	8	9	10	Ace
9	H	H	H	H	H	H	H	H	H	H
10	H	H	DD	DD	DD	DD	H	H	H	H
11	H	H	DD	DD	DD	DD	H	H	H	H
12	H	H	H	DD	DD	DD	H	H	H	H
13	H	H	H	H	S	H	H	H	H	H
14	H	H	S	S	S	H	H	H	H	H
15	S	S	S	S	S	H	H	H	H	H
16	S	S	S	S	S	H	H	H	H	SR
17	S	S	S	S	S	S	S	S	S	SR

SOFT HAND STRATEGY

VALUE OF THE DEALER'S UP CARD

YOUR HAND	2	3	4	5	6	7	8	9	10	Ace
Ace, 2	H	H	H	H	H	H	H	H	H	H
Ace, 3	H	H	H	H	H	H	H	H	H	H
Ace, 4	H	H	H	H	DD	H	H	H	H	H
Ace, 5	H	H	H	DD	DD	H	H	H	H	H
Ace, 6	H	H	H	DD	DD	H	H	H	H	H
Ace, 7	S	S	DD	DD	DD	S	S	H	H	H
Ace, 8	S	S	S	S	S	S	S	S	S	S
Ace, 9	S	S	S	S	S	S	S	S	S	S

PAIR SPLITTING STRATEGY

VALUE OF THE DEALER'S UP CARD

YOUR HAND	2	3	4	5	6	7	8	9	10	Ace
2 - 2	SPLIT	SPLIT	SPLIT	SPLIT	SPLIT	SPLIT	H	H	H	H
3 - 3	SPLIT	SPLIT	SPLIT	SPLIT	SPLIT	SPLIT	SPLIT	H	H	H
4 - 4	H	H	H	H	H	H	H	H	H	H
5 - 5	H	H	DD	DD	DD	DD	H	H	H	H
6 - 6	H	H	SPLIT	SPLIT	SPLIT	H	H	H	H	H
7 - 7	SPLIT	SPLIT	SPLIT	SPLIT	SPLIT	SPLIT	H	H	H	H
8 - 8	SPLIT	SPLIT	SPLIT	SPLIT	SPLIT	SPLIT	SPLIT	SPLIT	SPLIT	SR
9 - 9	S	SPLIT	SPLIT	SPLIT	SPLIT	S	SPLIT	SPLIT	S	S
10 - 10	S	S	S	S	S	S	S	S	S	S
ACE, ACE	SPLIT	SPLIT	SPLIT	SPLIT	SPLIT	SPLIT	SPLIT	SPLIT	SPLIT	SPLIT

LEGEND

HIT	H
STAND	S
DOUBLE DOWN	DD
SPLIT THE PAIR	SPLIT
SURRENDER	SR

FIGURE 13-2

benefit of my experience in practical play. This is why when you use the modified strategy in Figure 13-2, you'll see that I recommend a doubling action when you have a 12 against the dealer's up card of seven. I know it sounds crazy, but I've made that play so many times and have come out on top!

Key Points to Follow

1. Double-down rescue your 12-16 versus the dealer's 8-ace or your 17 versus ace.
2. Never split 4s, 5s, or face cards!
3. Use sound money management to determine your betting strategy.
4. Exercise complete discipline to set your high/low goal limits.
5. Find the casino with the best rules for optimum win.
6. Choose your table carefully—don't be in a hurry!
7. Try not to play with more than two other players at the table.
8. Never play when you are fatigued or tired.

PLAYING THE MATCH PLAY IN SPANISH 21

P laying the "match" in Spanish 21 is not the greatest bet to make. The house's edge on this type of bet is around –3%, which isn't terribly bad. But like anything else in gambling, it's subject to streaks and can be profitable if you apply some type of systematic approach to making your bets. In a six-deck configuration, the actual odds that you'll get an unsuited match are around 5.43:1, and around 12:1 for a suited match.

The match is paid 4:1 if any of your first two cards dealt matches the dealer's up card. It pays 9:1 if either of your cards not only matches the dealer's up card but is suited as well. For example, if one of your first two cards is a five of hearts and the dealer's up card is a five of spades, you are paid 4:1. If you have a five of hearts and the dealer has a five of hearts showing, you are paid 9:1, and so on. I've been dealt two sixes and the dealer had a six of diamonds. Of course I matched both cards to his, but also matched one of my sixes suited because it, too, was a six of diamonds. Therefore I was paid 4:1 on the unsuited six and 9:1 on the suited six.

To my knowledge there are no limits to how high you can make this wager as long as it does not exceed the table maximum. For example, you could make your regular Spanish 21 wager $25 and the match wager equal to, less than, or greater than $25—it's all up to you. These rules are most prevalent in the larger casinos and resorts. Some smaller local casinos (except those in Nevada) place limits on the match bet and in many cases won't allow you to play a match bet larger than your base bet. I do not recommend playing Spanish 21 tables where this rule exists.

If you're determined to play the match, then I suggest you wait for four to five initial deals where you haven't matched the dealer at all, and then begin a very small negative progression scheme, making use of the 4:1 and 9:1 odds this bet offers.

Figure 14-1 depicts the match strategy you may want to use if you're determined to play the match. This figure shows an ultraconservative negative betting schema that protects the player the most against the possibility of a sequence of thirteen no matches in a row. It's best used, and I stress this by going head-to-head one or two hands against the dealer, as in most of my strategies. In this particular one, you need at least $109 in order to see it through until the end. Even though you would make money at the 4:1 payoffs, what you're really hoping for are a few 9:1 suited match hits, which would really put you way out in front profit-wise.

In this figure you see ten columns that track your betting strategy:

Column 1: Assists you in tracking when you are beginning the strategy, *not* when you are beginning the betting!

Column 2: Tracks when you start making the real money bets.

Column 3: Tells you how much to bet in units when betting begins.

Column 4: Gives you your cumulative loss in units having lost all bets to that point.

MATCH PLAY BETTING SCHEMA (ULTRACONSERVATIVE)

COL 1 SEQ	COL 2 BET-NO	COL 3 BET-UNITS	COL 4 TOTAL NEG-BAL IF LOSS	COL 5 EXACT PAYOFF IF WIN AT 4:1	COL 6 EXACT PAYOFF IF WIN AT 9:1	COL 7 NET UNIT PROFIT GAIN 4:1	COL 8 NET UNIT PROFIT GAIN 9:1	COL 9 R.O.I. WAGERS AT 4:1	COL 10 R.O.I. WAGERS AT 9:1
WAIT-1	NO MATCH	0							
WAIT-2	NO MATCH	0							
WAIT-3	NO MATCH	0	0	0	0	0	0	0.00%	0.00%
WAIT-4	NO MATCH	0	0	0	0	0	0	0.00%	0.00%
WAIT-5	NO MATCH	0	0	0	0	0	0	0.00%	0.00%
6	1	1	1	4	9	4	9	300.00%	800.00%
7	2	1	2	4	9	3	8	100.00%	350.00%
8	3	1	3	4	9	2	7	33.33%	200.00%
9	4	2	5	8	18	5	15	60.00%	260.00%
10	5	2	7	8	18	3	13	14.29%	157.14%
11	6	3	10	12	27	5	20	20.00%	170.00%
12	7	4	14	16	36	6	26	14.29%	157.14%
13	8	6	20	24	54	10	40	20.00%	170.00%
14	9	8	28	32	72	12	52	14.29%	157.14%
15	10	11	39	44	99	16	71	12.82%	153.85%
16	11	16	55	64	144	25	105	16.36%	161.82%
17	12	22	77	88	198	33	143	14.29%	157.14%
18	13	32	109	128	288	51	211	17.43%	164.22%
TOTAL BET		109							

FIGURE 14-1

Column 5: If the bet is won, indicates how much you win at the 4:1 odds payoff.

Column 6: If the bet is won, indicates how much you win at the 9:1 odds payoff.

Column 7: Indicates, after winning this bet and after recouping all previous losses, how many units you will be ahead at the 4:1 payoff.

Column 8: Indicates, after winning this bet and after recouping all previous losses, how many units you will be ahead at the 9:1 payoff.

Column 9: Indicates, after making all wagers to this point and finally winning, what the exact R.O.I. (return on investment) is for a 4:1 winning. For example, on bet 12 the wager is 22 units; you lost 55 units before making this bet, so if you win the 4:1 payoff at this point you will be paid 88 units, thus yielding a 14.29% return, or a net 33 units for the 77 units invested.

Column 10: Indicates, after making all wagers to this point and finally winning, what the exact R.O.I. is for a 9:1 winning bet. For example, on bet 12 the wager is 22 units; you lost 55 units before making this bet, so if you win the 9:1 payoff at this point you will be paid 198 units, thus yielding a 157.14% return, or a net 143 units for the 77 units invested.

The idea here is to let the odds catch up with the probability of you not receiving any matching cards in five consecutive sets of initially dealt cards. So, according to Figure 14-1, you begin making bet 1 on sequence 6. Using the 4:1 and 9:1 odds payoffs, you can minimize your bet stepping and not get into a negative progression where you're doubling or more than doubling your bets from each bet to the next. At any point when you win you'll not only recoup all your previous losses but make a tidy return on the money you bet to that point.

It is also important to note that while I have played this game many times, I have noticed that when matches do come, they come in a series or clumped like this (Match means matched cards, NM means no match):

Match-Match
NM-NM-Match
NM-Match
NM-NM-NM-NM-NM-NM-Match
NM-Match

As you can see the matches sometimes come in strings and then nothing for long stretches. If you wait for five no matches to trigger the betting sequence, keep in mind that you may see a series of three out of five matches following your initial win. Therefore, you may want to accelerate your waiting scheme from five no-match waiting periods to only two, once the initial waiting of five no-match sequence hits and wins. It's one of those strange things like tie bets coming in a string in the game of baccarat. Ask any player who plays baccarat and she'll tell you that once a tie shows up, she'll bet the tie bet right afterward and usually win—I know I have. I think it has to with the great chaos theory, which has been postulated in recent years. No rhyme or reason—it just happens this way.

Please remember that the actual odds on the match bet are approximately 5.43:1, meaning you should match one out of every five to six hands! The following Figure 14-2 is designed for those of you who are a little more aggressive and want to maximize your return with a good bet on top once the match is hit. It is important to note that I've done some personal recordkeeping on the match bet and have determined that my winning opportunities in playing the match dramatically increase when I am going head-to-head against the dealer or playing with just one or two additional hands in the game. I rarely have to take the sequence past column 2, betting sequence 10, to hit it. On average, I hit the match every four to six hands, which clearly falls in line with the actual odds of hitting the unsuited match.

As you can see in Figure 14-2, you're now betting a sequence of 187 chips, which is a far cry from the 109 in Figure 14-1. As I've been saying throughout this book, you

MATCH PLAY BETTING SCHEMA (AGGRESSIVE)

COL 1 SEQ	COL 2 BET-NO	COL 3 BET-UNITS	COL 4 TOTAL NEG-BAL IF LCSS	COL 5 EXACT PAYOFF IF WIN AT 4:1	COL 6 EXACT PAYOFF IF WIN AT 9:1	COL 7 NET UNIT PROFIT GAIN 4:1	COL 8 NET UNIT PROFIT GAIN 9:1	COL 9 R.O.I. WAGERS AT 4:1	COL 10 R.O.I. WAGERS AT 9:1
WAIT-1	NO MATCH	0	0	0	0	0	0	0.00%	0.00%
WAIT-2	NO MATCH	0	0	0	0	0	0	0.00%	0.00%
WAIT-3	NO MATCH	0	0	0	0	0	0	0.00%	0.00%
WAIT-4	NO MATCH	0	0	0	0	0	0	0.00%	0.00%
WAIT-5	NO MATCH	0	0	0	0	0	0	0.00%	0.00%
6	1	1	1	4	9	4	9	300.00%	800.00%
7	2	1	2	4	9	3	8	100.00%	350.00%
8	3	2	4	8	18	6	16	100.00%	350.00%
9	4	2	6	8	18	4	14	33.33%	200.00%
10	5	3	9	12	27	6	21	33.33%	200.00%
11	6	5	14	20	45	11	36	42.86%	221.43%
12	7	9	23	36	81	22	67	56.52%	252.17%
13	8	11	34	44	99	21	76	29.41%	191.18%
14	9	15	49	60	135	26	101	22.45%	175.51%
15	10	20	69	80	180	31	131	15.94%	160.87%
16	11	28	97	112	252	43	183	15.46%	159.79%
17	12	38	135	152	342	55	245	12.59%	153.33%
18	13	52	187	208	468	73	333	11.23%	150.27%
TOTAL BET		187	187						

FIGURE 14-2

need to analyze your threshold of nervous tension, bankroll, and discipline to see a sequence like this one through. It is very easy to build your own progression schema; just be sure that when your bet finally hits you build some modicum of profit into it at the 4:1 payoff level. I suggest that if you can find a Spanish 21 game in your area, first stand behind someone playing the game and try this method fictitiously, playing the match even if the players aren't. See how many sequences it takes to make the match hit and win (just count the number of times the bet is made versus the times it actually wins, again on average—it should occur once out of every four to six hands). This should give you a little more confidence in this method before you actually employ it for real money—always a smart thing to do!

A quick story: I have an acquaintance whom I regularly see playing Spanish 21 when I frequent a certain casino in my area; we'll call him "Double Down," a nickname we assigned him jokingly. Anyway, one day he walked in and stopped to say hello to me while I was playing at a regular blackjack game, then proceeded to the Spanish 21 game. He usually buys in for around $50 and plays the $5 tables. I finished up at my table and began watching him play. He religiously plays the match bet and was at the table by himself. Once I stepped up, he had hit a "suited" match bet for 9:1, with $10 bet (a $90 payoff), then proceeded to consistently hit a match every couple of hands throughout the shoe. By the time the dust settled after that shoe was over, I estimate that he made a whopping $560 just on the match bet portion of play in just *one shoe* playing $5 and $10 bets . . . incredible! Most people you will see play the match bet always wait to play when there are either no people or possibly just one player at the table; they know that their odds of hitting the match are much greater when they are getting a greater distribution of or access to the cards in the shoe—a smart move when playing this option.

Tips to Stay in and with the Game

In this chapter, I assemble all the best advice I can muster to keep you in good form no matter what the circumstances. This isn't betting or strategy advice. This is good old common-sense advice on how to handle yourself and others in the casino, and how to manage yourself and your own expectations.

What to Do When the Cards Change

Whether you go head-to-head against the dealer or play with a couple of others at the table, at some point, all of a sudden you will experience the cards totally change. One minute you're playing great, maybe winning and losing about even or maybe winning a little more than usual, making your double downs and splits, and then all of a sudden the dealer never breaks. You lose four straight hands, win one, lose six straight hands, and then the dealer starts getting blackjacks and everything goes wrong. So, how do you combat this scenario? The simple answer is, leave the table. I do not endorse your continuing, but if you are hell-bent on staying, then you can try adding one or two more hands to play at the table. In other words, if you're playing one hand, begin playing two and so on. Casinos set a premium for doing this, usually double the table minimum for an extra place to bet, three times the table minimum for three spots, and so on. This moves the winning hands away from the dealer and back into one of the player's spots. If by chance this strategy works, and many times it does, stay with this type of play as you continue to win consistently, but go back to one hand once the cards turn again—but not before! If a bad situation persists, never try to slug it out with fate, the cards, or the dealer because the house always wins when you try. Just leave, get your composure back, have a drink to take the edge off, and relax for twenty to thirty minutes; then try again once you're stabilized.

Bring Enough Cash to Stay in the Game

Having enough cash during a session is so critical. Most people do not bring enough cash to withstand a really bad series of losing hands, and it simply wipes out their bankroll. That's why it is essential to bring the session money packets I talked about in Chapter 7. Give yourself a chance to win! You can't expect to start playing and not experience a series of losses every now and then. Even the best of players experience losing streaks from a starting point. It happens, and there's no getting around it. Understand that to win you need betting and playing strategy, but you can't be really successful unless you have patience and discipline as well. It's when you become impatient, compounded with being low on session money (underfunded), that you'll always take it in the shorts—every time, *guaranteed*.

People believe they can go to a casino with $100 and make $1,000 in an afternoon or evening. I'm flat-out telling you that it almost never happens and is extremely difficult to do. If a person is very lucky once in his life at the tables it might happen, but to do it with any kind of consistency, you can bet it won't happen, not in one sitting!

The absolute worst thing you can do is buy in for chips at $100, lose that, buy in for another $50 (thinking you'll get the hundred back), lose that, and buy in for 20 bucks (in a last-ditch effort to bring things around), and lose that as well! Casinos love to see folks do this, so don't be one of them. This action is called "chipping yourself away." Don't be a victim of your own stupidity. In Chapter 7 I gave you the minimum formula for buying into a game.

That formula was derived from literally hundreds of sessions of play. Follow the old cliché: Do it right, or don't do it at all. There's a lot of merit in that statement.

Common-Sense Rules to Follow When Playing for Real Money

Here's a group of things you really need to pay attention to, whether you're playing as a recreational player or as a professional. All these issues are pretty cardinal in gaming in general.

Don't Play When You're Rushed

So many folks walk into a casino, plop down some buy-in money, and believe they're going to make a quick killing before going home for dinner, or before heading for an appointment, or before picking up the kids, or before taking a flight out of town—you get the picture. Not giving yourself enough time is a recipe for disaster. Why? Because when you walk into a casino, you never know what's going to happen, and you need to stay for as long as it takes. Sure, you could get lucky and make a quick killing at the tables, but that doesn't happen with any degree of frequency. The point is, you're already under enough pressure concentrating on how to play the cards and devising your betting strategy while watching the cards fall, that you don't need the added pressure of trying to make a quick profit before going somewhere. It's absolutely ridiculous, but many folks rush themselves. That just gives the casinos more leverage against them!

Here's a story to illustrate this rule. My girlfriend and I flew to Oakland and then drove up to Tahoe. We were tired and wanted to rest after the four-hour trip through the snow and rain. Once rested, we were raring to go downstairs to eat and then try our luck at the tables. She's one of those women who loves to get all dolled up before being anywhere, so consequently I was ready at least twenty minutes before she was. Instead of waiting in the room I decided to go downstairs and have a drink. She agreed to meet me in the bar and down I went. When I arrived on the casino floor, the smell of money was in the air. I walked by a $5 blackjack table with only one guy sitting there, watched a couple of minutes, I then decided "What the heck, I've got a few minutes to burn!" You guessed it. I plopped down about $150 and began to play, all the while checking my watch. Ten minutes went by and I was down about fifty bucks; five minutes after that I was down about a hundred bucks. Looking at my watch again I knew she'd be there at any moment. Feeling totally crazed, knowing I was down too much for the session, I made one last bet with the remainder of my session money, which was forty-five bucks. Let's just say that was the most expensive drink I never had the pleasure of drinking.

Never Gamble with a Companion Who Doesn't Like Gambling

Why would I mention this? Because it's another needless pressure you shouldn't be handling while gambling. The last thing you need while you're focused and making money is someone saying, "Honey, can we stop this now? I'm tired and want to go to bed," or "Look, babe, I didn't come to Vegas to watch you gamble all day and all night. Hurry up because I want to go to the shopping boutiques in the casino." If you've ever been gaming in Las Vegas, Atlantic City, Lake Tahoe, Reno, or wherever, you heard those "calls to doom," haven't you? From now on, gamble alone or with someone who is as committed to the game as you are!

Never Gamble When You're Tired

So many of us do just that. Here we are, it's 4:00 A.M., we've been up since 10:00 A.M. the previous morning, we can barely keep our eyes open, and we're playing for *real money!* What's wrong with this picture? Your nerves are shot, your judgment is definitely impaired; your spouse or significant other is mad because you aren't with him or her in the hotel room; you may have had a few drinks too many; you're feeling really "rummy"; and the casino vultures are circling over your table waiting for you to capitulate. Need I say more? Yes, it's another recipe for doom, so just don't do it! When gambling, you should be refreshed and invigorated.

I remember when I was gambling pseudo professionally, my best times at the tables took place when I got up, showered, took my time getting dressed, ate breakfast in a leisurely manner, read the newspaper in my room, and strolled around the casino property relaxed and not in a hurry to be anywhere. I kept my gaming sessions to a strict predetermined profit goal and then relaxed in one of the luxurious bars, sipping tea or coffee and watching the cabaret, the football game, or just the people walking by, until I was ready to start the next session.

Never Gamble on a Budget or with Sacred Cash

Don't gamble with money you don't really have. That is to say, don't borrow from savings or use money earmarked for something else important. Bring enough money to endure the battle and bring money you can afford to lose, not money that is sacred to your needs for your livelihood or that of your family.

Never Gamble at a Table with Folks Who Irritate You

Keeping positive and focused requires all your concentration; therefore, it is essential that you minimize all possible distractions and negative influences while you're in the game.

People who irritate you have an impact on your playing acumen—you can count on it. If there are people who, in your opinion, are not hitting the cards right, leave. If there are people who are smoking and you hate smoke, leave. If a person joins the game obviously drunk, and you're appalled by public drunkenness, leave. If people are whining, leave. If for any reason someone or something bothers you—you guessed it—leave. Find another game at another table or at another casino. Besides, you should be looking for games where you can get a head-to-head game against the dealer anyway.

Never Keep Lots of Cash on You

Casinos have great deposit/credit systems in place and you should use them. If you can, have all funds (called front money) wired to the casino where you'll be staying. Upon arrival, visit the cashier's cage and the cashier will set you up with a special ID card to be used for drawing credit markers at the tables against the deposit you wired. Upon leaving the table, take only the chips that you want to cash in. Push the rest back to the dealer for redeposit into your account, and one of the floor supervisors will give you a receipt. Never allow folks to see you cash in large quantities of chips because you're inviting trouble and exposing yourself to unnecessary risk. The cash you take back to your room should always be minimal. Most casino resorts provide safes in their hotel rooms or at the registration desk, and I fully endorse you using one for your cash and jewelry. For those of you gambling close to home, have the casino draw you a check so you don't walk into a parking lot carrying thousands in cash. You never know who's been watching you cash out. Or have someone from security escort you to your car; otherwise you're asking for trouble! If you're driving a car, always use the valet service when going from casino to casino. There's nothing like door-to-door service to ensure that you're never too far away from casino security. Remember, it pays big dividends to play it safe.

Use a Playing and Betting Strategy and Stick with It

Now you have the strategies down cold, you've been practicing, and you've had a couple of moderately successful journeys to a local casino, or just went to watch. You've practiced at home some of the betting strategies we've talked about, or possibly you've constructed some variations of your own that you prefer, which is totally okay. What is essential is having a strategy to use *before* walking in to the casino. Have all your key decisions made before getting there! Write them down on a piece of paper if you have to, just to keep yourself honest to you! No decisions going in, means no money coming out, and that's for certain—the casino will grind you to dust every time you try to wing it. The reason you have to employ a strategy is so that you don't second-guess yourself at the tables. The last thing you want to feel like is a yo-yo, psyching yourself out by see-sawing on strategies trying to guess correctly. Use a strategy and stick with it!

Set Your Win/Loss Limits to Match Your Bankroll

Here's a story that illustrates this rule. Recently I was gaming at a local casino in the greater Seattle area. A gentleman I had met on earlier trips walked in while I was playing some Spanish 21—I'll call him "the doctor" for this illustration. As usual, he headed for the cash machine, drew about $1,000, and came to the table. He began betting $100 chips, the table maximum for this casino, and began going up and down like an elevator. He bet one position, then two positions, doubled and split when appropriate, and so on. At times he was ahead about $600, then hit a rough streak, and have only $400 in front of him. This went on for about an hour and a half until finally he bet his last black chip (a $100 chip) and went bust. Now, for the doctor to do this was evidently no big deal because he was widely known in the casino as a high roller, so losing a thousand bucks for him was no big deal.

While I was watching him destroy his buy-in stake, I was thinking someone should teach this guy a money management system, because if he had one, he'd make a killing almost every time. You can probably see what the problems were from the start. First, he was betting the table maximum, allowing no room to vary his bet upward at any point. Second, if he was planning on betting the table maximum, he didn't bring enough cash to the table to withstand even a moderate losing streak. He simply wiped out with only an initial ten $100 chips to play with. At minimum, he should have had at least $4,000 in front of him, if not more. Think about this: If the doctor had taken his original $1,000 and turned it into $25 chips, instead of $100 chips, he'd have had plenty of buy-in chips to maneuver through the game, bet a decent one- to four-unit spread, and certainly would have been able to withstand any short downturn in the game. The moral of this story is, bring enough cash to weather the storm and have it coincide with your betting unit values and session packets.

Play Single or Double Deck If You Have the Choice

If you can't find single- or double-deck configurations in your area, find the most favorable configuration that you can. Do try to stay away from eight-deck shoe configurations if at all possible. Don't ask me why, but I've never been very successful at playing against this configuration. There are too many chances that the high or low cards get clumped and literally bury you at the game. It always seems as though the dealer gets a ten card up and you're forever trying to beat the dealer's possible twenty. It's the absolute worst. Single- or double-deck configurations are much preferred. Although shuffling occurs more often, you'll have a more even distribution of wins and losses, making our CLB strategy extremely useful, especially if you're going head-to-head against the dealer. The odds are quite high that you will not lose more than four to five in a row using the CLB strategies discussed in Chapters 9 and 10.

Play at a Casino That Offers What You Like

Find the best conditions that you desire, and settle for nothing less! If you have a favorite establishment that has the liberal rules you like to play, go there, and make yourself happy walking in the door. If you have befriended the personnel and they enjoy seeing you when you come to play, all the better; not all casino personnel consider skilled players marks or suckers. If it's your preference, find a table with no players or a table with no more than one other player; select third or first base, if available. If you enjoy going head-to-head against the dealer, find a table that allows you that option. In other words, find the perfect scenario that appeals to you. Never compromise, especially when gambling in cities like Las Vegas, Tahoe, Reno, or even Atlantic City; there are just too many tables and variations out there to compromise yourself.

A great example of playing at an establishment with the right kind of options in Las Vegas, for example, are casinos located in the downtown area of the city. At some of them you can split aces and pairs as many times as you want, and here's the really great one—you can double down after receiving more than two cards—*wow!* Plus, drawing any six cards to a total of 21 or less automatically wins! Now those are what I call rules a player should look for. It's obvious why the smaller casinos have those rules; they need to compete for the business that the Vegas strip hotels have taken from the downtown area. In any event, local casinos in each state and city are constantly trying to compete with one another offering bonus hands, match play coupons, special cash drawings on the off days when business isn't as brisk—you get the idea. Again, always try to find rules and special nuances that benefit you, the player.

Gamble in the Early-Morning Hours

Most of the better players come out between 1:00 and 3:00 A.M. Why? To minimize negative influences that could potentially affect their game. Fewer folks at the table means more control. No drunks, no inexperienced players playing incorrectly, lower noise levels with fewer folks around, not as many slot machines going *ding, ding, ding* and *bong, bong, bong*, all in all add up to a more relaxed environment. Remember to always try to find a table where you can play two positions (double the table minimum to do this) and not get too anxious about the cash you have out there. Therefore, if you are a $5 bettor, then try to find a $5 table; betting two positions means you're betting $10 per position or $20 total. If this makes you uncomfortable, then try and find a $3 table. Just try to be flexible enough to bet two positions when you have to, and try not to be nervous about doing it. By playing in the early-morning hours, your chance of finding lower limit tables with no players is optimal, and you can play several hours without being hindered by inexperienced players jumping in and out of the game. Going to higher limit tables ($15 and greater), you are almost assured of being alone and unhindered.

Exercise Discipline and Patience

Use total and complete discipline and patience. Don't make any "Hail Mary" bets! These are bets way higher than your normal bet spread you'd use when trying to get even. Remember, playing 21 takes all kinds of patience, and trying to force the win usually won't work. Follow the game and analyze what's going on. Don't lose your cool if things go badly. If the positive play isn't happening, take a break, find another table, or leave the casino. Remember, you're the one in control—don't let the game control you! Don't get into a 21 trance and be oblivious to all the losses. Pay attention at all times to what's happening at your table, watch the other players, watch the cards, watch the dealer, watch the shuffles, watch everything! If things don't go as planned, remember, nobody wins all the time, not even me, so when Lady Luck turns against you, just get up and leave, and remember, tomorrow is another day! I see so many folks get to 200% of 400% of buy-in, making the grade, never having it so good, and then they slide back down to 100% of buy-in or below, and refuse to leave with a profit. It's absolutely unbelievable!

Here's a quick story. A friend of mine, we'll call him Hank, was playing Spanish 21 one day. He bought in for $75 and in less than forty minutes he accumulated almost $285 in profits, which is almost 300% over buy-in! You can see this coming, can't you? The cards went really sour when another friend of ours jumped into the game. Totally oblivious to what was going on, meaning he didn't realize that the extra hand in the game rotated the winning hands to the dealer's position, he let his profits slide to just over $85 over buy-in, or slightly more than 100% in profits. He switched tables to play double deck and, yes, the slide continued. He caught a short streak and won over $115, bringing him to almost 200% of buy-in. He wouldn't stop playing. I finally told him that if he didn't quit I'd throw handcuffs on him. I kept on him about the rules of leaving, which, by the way, he knew very well was a big sticking point for me. I was finally able to convince him to stop, but as you can very well see, he exercised no discipline. If he would have "locked up" his profits at the eighteen- to twenty-unit goal right from the start at the Spanish 21 table, and just kept playing his initial streak, putting away 50% of each winning hand into the "locked-up" money pool, he would have kept the entire $285 protected against any kind of slide into the negative. This would have saved him playing time, undue stress, and brought him a great feeling of satisfaction having conquered the gambling bug and the mindless addiction that occurs when things start going topsy-turvy. Please don't let this be you. Try to place whatever safeguard mechanisms into place to ensure that when goals are met, high or low, the discipline you show always makes you a winner.

Blackjack Tournaments 16

What's surprising is that many intermediate to serious players, for whom this book is written, have never tried playing in a blackjack tournament. I suspect it's because many of these major tournaments occur in Las Vegas, Atlantic City, Reno, or Tahoe, and when folks visit these places, they are surely not coming to play tournaments. But with the change of federal laws over the last ten to twelve years allowing Indian casinos to proliferate, many tribal casinos and locally regulated casinos in almost thirty-eight states have launched their own series of tournaments to get the general public interested in playing table games, especially blackjack and Spanish 21. Many folks are still intimidated by these table games—they look too difficult, too busy, too expensive, too everything, which we know really isn't true. Tournaments are a great way for casinos to get folks to learn the games without fearing they may lose their mortgage playing them. Most casinos have tournament directors who are more than happy to instruct new players on the game and how the tournaments work, making the entire experience a fun one for the newcomers.

Why Do Casinos Offer Tournaments?

Besides getting folks interested in playing blackjack or Spanish 21, the main reason casinos sponsor tournaments is to attract players to the live-action tables. While tournament players wait for their rounds of play to come up, casino managers want these players to play on the live-action tables. To attract tournament players, casinos offer generous jackpots to those individuals who finish in the top three or four positions, anywhere from $500 to $3,000 nightly jackpots. These jackpots have really become serious marketing tools for casinos to attract players. Obviously, those casinos directly competing with others in their immediate area will try to draw tournament players with any type of gimmick they can, from offering tournament participants free food, free additional match-play gaming coupons, travel escapes, teddy bears, free spins on the pari-mutuel wheels, you name it.

How Do Tournaments Work, and Are There Different Types?

Most tournaments work this way: Entrants register at a signup desk and pay a buy-in fee, usually anywhere between $10 for a $500 tournament, up to $25 for a tournament that offers a potential jackpot of $1,000 to $3,000. Players sit at a regulation blackjack or Spanish 21 table with the maximum number of players that the table will hold, which is generally six to seven. The dealer issues around 500 to 1,000 tournament chips per player depending on the type of tournament being played. The first round is the qualifying round and generally lasts about fifteen to twenty-five deals to the players, or the equivalent of thirty to forty minutes of play. The tournament director generally takes the two highest chip count holders and advances them into a semifinal round.

To those players who don't qualify in the first round, these tournaments usually offer what is called a re-buy round.

A re-buy round generally costs about 50% of what the original buy-in did, but it varies from tournament to tournament. Once these players re-buy, they play another qualifying round to get into the semifinal round. The tournament director usually takes two to three people from the re-buy round and advances them to the semifinal round. The play remains the same for subsequent rounds.

The betting maximums are usually from 5 to 500 or 5 to 1,000 in the qualifying rounds and generally go up to 25 to 1,000 in semifinal and final rounds. Please note that I've purposely omitted the dollar signs from the bet amounts because players are betting chips representing dollar equivalent units and the object is to accumulate as many units (chips) as you can during the round of play. Some tournaments allow players to bet all they have in front of them, so consequently, if you are issued 1,000 in chips and build your stake up to 2,250, you can theoretically bet the entire 2,250 in one bet as a last desperate or ambitious move for the last hand of play, or any hand of play, for that matter.

Additionally, in the spirit of fairness, during each deal the person dealt to first is rotated, starting at position number one (the first seat to the dealer's left) on hand number one, and moves into the next position around the table for every subsequent deal. No one is allowed to bet until the first person has bet; then the next person bets, and on down the line. Once a bet has been placed, it can't be changed or adjusted in any way.

There are numerous types of tournaments. Some offer a nightly jackpot only, while others offer a nightly jackpot plus a big granddaddy jackpot that follows in a month, a quarter, semiannually, or something like that, which is open to the nightly finalists. These jackpots are considerable, usually $10,000 to $1,000,000. The million-dollar tournament is quite notable and is held by one of the larger casinos in Las Vegas.

Becoming a savvy tournament player could pay off in big dividends once you've honed your skills. Playing a blackjack tournament is one of the best bets in the house! Where else can you pay an average buy-in of $20 and have a better than even chance to win nightly jackpots that range between $500 and $3,000 at your local casinos? It's a great proposition, plus tournaments are always really fun and you generally meet lots of folks who have the same gaming interests that you do.

These tournaments are held in various "flavors" as well. You have your normal blackjack tournament consisting of play very similar to six- and eight-deck shoes, and the only difference is that a natural blackjack (an initially dealt two-card 21) payoff is usually 2:1, not 3:2. This ratio is different because tournament chips don't come in 50 cent and $1 units; they come usually in 5, 25, 100, and 500 denomination sizes.

Then there are Spanish 21 tournaments, which are generally played with six- to eight-deck shoes and the only difference is the optional match play. I've designed and played these Spanish 21 tournaments and believe me when I say they are the most exciting because of the match play! Your bankroll can be really down, and then you hit a suited match play bet (pays 9:1), with 50 units up, and all of a sudden you're a serious contender, having just won 450 units. When this happens to you during your round of play, trust me when I say that it provides a very palpable level of excitement; at any moment, during any round, someone can propel him- or herself into serious contention. Spanish 21 tournaments are a real gas!

There's also a new type of tournament that I developed for a casino, called the Face-Off Challenge. This tournament pits the player against the dealer head-to-head for twenty-five hands double-deck, which is equivalent to about six minutes of play. The player receives 1,000 units for playing; natural blackjacks pay 2:1, and the bet structure is minimum 5 units to unlimited. The player is allowed to play one, two, three, and up to seven positions if he or she wants to; however, each position played counts as a hand dealt against the twenty-five hands set for the tournament. This particular tournament challenges serious players in every way possible—

playing strategy, betting strategy, discipline—and you have only twenty-five hands to show everyone the stuff you are made of. This particular style of tournament is really well suited for the CLB strategies contained in this book because the player has all the control: No one else gets better cards, no one else splits cards that shouldn't be split, and the player has great control in adding and subtracting hands against the dealer.

What's the Playing Strategy for Tournaments?

Playing a tournament with other players is different from playing on live tables because tournament players are actually playing against each other at the table. The player's goal is to achieve a chip total at the end of the round that's higher than all others at the table This sometimes drives a player to make some very unorthodox plays. For example, if the player to your left is doubling on an 11 with a big bet up and you have a pair of ten cards, you might split those tens in hopes of taking possibly a ten card away from the other player, lessening his or her chances of achieving 21. Or you might be down on your total chip count on the very last hand of the round and in order to win you need an additional margin of victory; therefore, if you were dealt a pair of sixes against the dealer's seven through nine, you might consider a split in order to double your bet and catch up with players who are ahead in chip totals and have already completed their hands. Or instead of taking just a hit, you double down to attain the margin you need to stay in it. You'll find yourself making some wacky plays during a tournament that you would never consider making on a live table. Basically, anything goes in a tournament, and it's total pandemonium sometimes; however, that doesn't mitigate the need for following the guidelines of basic strategy as the template for your play. But sometimes deviation is necessary to reaching the unit goal. It's a form of gambling, right?

Tournament Betting Strategies

Here's where you can really test the strategies I've shown you without really getting hurt at all. The most you can lose is your buy-in money, and that's generally not very significant. Tournament play is a great way of getting used to and modifying some betting levels as certain playing and losing conditions start occurring. In addition to what you've already learned, here are three more betting strategies that many use somewhat effectively for tournament play. It is important to note that tournaments, as stated earlier, are usually only fifteen to twenty-five hands—therefore, any betting strategy has limitations simply based on the fact that not enough hands are being dealt to work through the strategy.

The Front Game Player

This type of strategy is used by many aggressive players who take the attitude that they will bet very high in the beginning hands in the hopes of breaking the game wide open. For example, let's say you're playing a standard 21 tournament where the betting levels are 5 to 500 units per hand on any qualifying round. Each player is issued 500 tournament chips. The front game player plays something like this: She'll open with a seventy-five-unit bet instead of the average ten- to fifteen-unit bet, and if she wins, she will press her bets a little higher for the next hand, possibly to 100 or even 125 units, similar to the profit takedown strategy in Chapter 10. If this hand wins she will increase again another 25% to 40%, and so on. At any time she loses, she will drop down to the seventy-five-unit bet or possibly even fifty-unit and try again. Her goal, of course is this: By winning her hands, she places a psychological strain on the other players, making them feel as though they need to bet higher in order to keep pace with her. A secondary motive is to break the game wide open by getting so far ahead that no one will be able to catch her and keep the game out of reach. Believe me when I say sometimes it really works! Players have used this strategy against me, and it does place a tremendous amount of stress on me and the other players, especially when this type of player gets a black-jack. As you'll recall, tournament blackjacks normally pay 2:1, making it extremely difficult to catch a player who has almost double what she was issued just on the first four hands played. This type of player can now just bet the minimum, stay on cruise control for the remainder of the shoe if desired, and still remain in serious contention at the end of the round. This type of player is very tough to beat if she's hitting better than a 60% average in winning hands.

The Extreme Front Game Player

I really love to see this type of player in the game! This is a player who has an attitude of "I'm either going to make it or break it, right out of the gate!" Now, I respect that type of attitude, and here's why: Tournaments take usually two to four hours to play on average, depending on the number of entrants, and a player has to make it through three rounds of play, sometimes four if you count a re-buy round. That's a serious commitment in time if, in fact, the player doesn't end up finishing in the money. The extreme front player is the person who, when issued 500 units in chips, either goes all in (that's an expression in blackjack meaning you bet all that's in front of you) or bets at least 250 units, or half of what is in front of him, all on the first hand! This is indeed a gutsy move, but in many cases pays off in a big way! If this player wins on the initial hand, he is so far ahead of everyone else that he certainly has room on subsequent hands to be very aggressive and stretch his lead even more with very little risk to his bankroll. I've battled these players, and it's very tough, even for me, as competitive as I am, to compete with this very bold strategy. On the flip side, if the extreme front game player goes all in and loses, that's it folks; he's out of the round right away and it's off to the re-buy round. If he goes in only 50%, 250 units, and loses, he still has one more chance to come even with a second huge 250-unit win, and can try the sequence all over again. This is an extreme move, but if it works, he is definitely in the chips. Another downside to this strategy is that if the player receives a doubling or splitting hand, he has no options if he went all in initially. The 50%, or 250 unit, player does have the option and will more than likely take it, but if this player loses, then it's off to the re-buy round for him as well.

The Back Game Player

About 25% of the folks who play tournaments fall into this category. This type of player plays only the minimum bet or twice the minimum bet. This player will play 5- and 10-size units and lurk in the background hoping for the front or extreme front players to lose their lead or accumulated edge (bankroll), and this does often happen. The back game player usually waits until the last three or four hands of the round before making his or her move—often it's during the second to the last or the very last hand. The move this player usually makes is very calculated, because he or she is always very cognizant of each player's skill and tendencies in betting. You'll often find that many players who play any variation of the front game feel as though they are invincible and very frequently do lose their edge. When this happens they're terribly demoralized and start making decisions based on sheer emotion rather than strategy. The back game players love it when this happens because they've played extremely conservatively and are still in touch with their strategy and always ready to capitalize on the front player's weakness. The downside to back game–playing strategy is this: If the back game player has been getting relatively good cards throughout the shoe or possibly in the first half of the shoe, he or she now risks getting bad cards during the last hands, making huge bets very risky. The central focus of a back game player is to always stay in the strike zone, so to speak. Always stay within a bankroll range to potentially amass a formidable challenge to all players during the second to the last or the last hand of the round.

Partnering with Someone to Form a Team

Because playing a tournament is such a commitment in time, not to mention energy since you may be battling it out with as many as seventy players in an evening, sometimes it makes sense to form a partnership with someone whose skill you respect and admire. In doing so you almost double your chances of taking some money home for your efforts at the end of an evening. It basically works like this: You both agree to split whatever is won. If both or either one of you end up finishing in the money, then you total up the winnings and split them. Remember, tournament play is playing against others at the table, not against the house! You have to be shrewd, clever, and calculated to be a player who continually finishes in one of the top slots each and every week. I can assure you that once folks see how well you do on a continual basis, believe me, they will approach you to become a team player. Make sure to be selective; watch others play carefully and assess their skill. One thing you don't want is to finish in the money more often than your teammate and end up sharing your proceeds much more often than your teammate shares with you! The partnership must be fair and equitable. You can now see how important it is that you respect the skill of your teammate.

Taking Insurance on Dealer's Aces in Tournaments

If you are dealt a natural blackjack during play and the tournament in which you are playing pays initial blackjacks at a rate of 2:1, and the dealer's up card is an ace, *always* take insurance against the dealer having a blackjack. Here's why. Suppose you bet 50 units, get a blackjack, and the dealer gets an ace. If you place a twenty-five-unit insurance bet and the dealer has a blackjack, then you'd get paid 2:1 on your insurance bet, which is fifty units. If you push or tie the dealer on your blackjack, you'll net fifty units for this play. If the dealer doesn't have the blackjack, you'll lose the twenty-five units on your insurance bet but win 2:1 on your blackjack, netting you seventy-five units for the play, which is still 150% of your original bet. Many folks do not realize the value of this strategic play, which should always be leveraged in this situation. This play, of course, does not apply in Spanish 21 because you are always immediately paid on any 21 that you receive.

How Tough Can It Get in a Tournament?

The answer is, *real tough*. I've been in tournaments where I've won only two hands out of twenty. You're probably asking yourself "How is that possible?" Let me tell you, it certainly is possible. You realize, of course, that theoretically you should be winning at least 4.7 hands out of ten, or 47%, right? Then you can surmise that on average you should win about eight to nine hands out of the maximum twenty hands dealt in a tournament, right? Therefore, to win only two to three hands over twenty hands of play is way below the average, and how could anyone sustain those kinds of losses? Using the CLB strategy, of course! The CLB strategy has saved my butt on more than one occasion when this situation has occurred. Not only did it save my hide, but in two cases I was actually a qualifying round winner.

Here's an example. I went from the initial 500-unit issue down to a 340-unit balance by the seventh hand. I won the eighth hand, which brought me back up to a balance of 485 units. Then I lost through the fourteenth hand, bringing me to a balance of 400 units. Then I won the fifteenth hand, which brought me back up to 480 units, and I'm still in the hunt. I got to the final hand, and had to deviate from the CLB strategy because it's basically do or die at this point. After scrutinizing and assessing the bankrolls of my three other competitors, I determined what the odds would be of finishing in the money betting certain amounts. I finally figured that betting 150 units might put me in at least second place, allowing me to leave back 290 units, beating the leader who at one point had 1,375 units at the thirteenth hand and finished out the round with only 225 units in front of her. Hey, it goes that way sometimes.

The key element here is that the CLB strategy can really work when you experience a tournament or live-action round sequence like this:

Lose-Lose-Lose-Lose-Lose-Lose-Lose-Win
Lose-Lose-Lose-Lose-Lose-Lose-Win
Lose-Lose-Lose-Lose-Win (end of the round)

Looks frightening, doesn't it? Only three wins out of twenty, yet I was one of four people left on the table when the final hand was played, and all the remaining players, at one point or another, had bankrolls that exceeded 700 units! Hard to fathom, isn't it? Figure 16-1 shows what it looked like in a formalized run format.

This is a classic case of CLB strategy in action and of the frontrunners thinking they were invincible. Just think about it—one of the players was up to over 1,300 units and finished with only 225! She was so far ahead, and all she had to do was bet the minimum and she would have been the winner of the round by a long shot. The problem was, she made a couple of really big bets once she reached that 1,300-unit threshold and then lost. She tried to recoup with a few more bigger bets, which again lost, and finally she tanked most of her bankroll in the final hands. As for me, as Figure 16-1 indicates, I stayed in it right up to the nineteenth hand, where I then strayed from CLB because the twentieth hand is the last hand. I had to make a sizable bet of 150 units, which allowed me to hold back the 290 units, to at least finish in the second spot if two out of the three players busted. As it turned out, I

TOURNAMENT RUN FROM MONDAY, AUGUST 19, 2002

HAND NO.	BET CODE	BET AMT	RESULT	GAIN/LOSS	RUNNING BALANCE	CLB ACCRUAL
INITIAL	W1	$5	L	($5)	($5)	($5)
2	L2	$5	L	($5)	($10)	($10)
3	L3	$10	L	($10)	($20)	($20)
4	L4	$15	L	($15)	($35)	($35)
5	L5	$5	L	($5)	($40)	($40)
6	L6 CLB1	$44	L	($44)	($84)	($84)
7	L7 CLB2	$76	L	($76)	($160)	($160)
8	L7 CLB2	$145	WIN	$145	($15)	$0
9	W9	$5	L	($5)	($20)	($5)
10	L2	$5	L	($5)	($25)	($10)
11	L3	$10	L	($10)	($35)	($20)
12	L4	$15	L	($15)	($50)	($35)
13	L5	$5	L	($5)	($55)	($40)
14	L6 CLB1	$45	L	($45)	($100)	($84)
15	L7 CLB2	$75	WIN	$75	($25)	$0
16	W9	$5	L	($5)	($30)	($5)
17	L2	$5	L	($5)	($35)	($10)
18	L3	$10	L	($10)	($45)	($20)
19	L4	$15	L	($15)	($60)	($35)
20	LAST HAND	$150	WIN	$150	$90	$0

FIGURE 16-1

was victorious—two of three other players busted out and the third miscalculated his final bet and I beat him by 5 units. Now that's what I call luck!

It All Comes Down to the Last Hand

When playing tournaments you really have to be something akin to a military strategist, especially on the last hand of the round. I've seen so many folks in fifth or sixth position conservatively play 50% to 75% of their final bankroll and win the last round because they anticipated and scrutinized everyone else's final bankroll and bet. After analyzing all the possible outcomes, these folks stay in contention as top players in the round. Please understand that in many cases a player would win the final round anyway if he or she received a blackjack, and subsequently doubled the last wager, putting that player on top. But also in many cases, a player keeps enough in reserve to stay in contention in the event he or she loses. The key to winning in tournaments is being able to assess the probabilities of the people in the lead going into the final hand, busting out their hands, and not having enough reserve bankroll to stay in contention on the final chip count. It's a real chess game to be sure.

Most tournament directors will mandate a total chip count for each player at the table before the final hand in order to let the other players know how much their opponents have in front of them. What sometimes makes the last hand difficult is, if you're dealt, you're forced to set the initial bet on the table, allowing others to scrutinize your bankroll and adjust their bet accordingly.

What *Not* to Do When Playing in Blackjack Tournaments

As you become better acquainted with playing, there will be times when you get fed up with the hands you're getting, while other players are getting two, three, even four black-jacks during the round, and you're getting *bupkas*. Never lose your cool and begin making "Hail Mary" bets trying to punch out the win or to catch up with the others. Sure, there will be a time toward the end of the round, if you are trailing two to three players who are ahead of you by at least a three to one margin, that you'll have to become bold, but I don't recommend making such big moves unless you're three hands or closer to the end of the round. If you're trailing by a large margin, it's never a good idea to go all in before the second-to-last or last hand of the round. And when you do make that kind of move, make sure that you always leave something in reserve for a doubling or splitting opportunity.

Playing tournaments is really great not only for developing your playing and betting skills but also developing your attitude and overall view of how other players affect you during play. Tournaments are also great social events, much like any other league or sport you might participate in. I guarantee that you'll have great fun playing in them and certainly you'll meet some nice folks in the process who share the same passion as you do for the game. But the greatest benefit you'll derive from playing tournaments is that you'll get the experience of using the strategies contained in this book, and, of course, you'll develop that very necessary ingredient—discipline!

THE READINESS REVIEW—
YOUR CHECKLIST FOR SUCCESS!

W̲e have, as many would say, reached the moment of truth. If you have read this far you have undoubtedly been examining several of the strategies in this book from sheer curiosity. Time now to begin the process of readying yourself for the battles and victories that are sure to come your way! Here is your checklist for success:

1.   Read this book completely at least two times and mark the sections where the strategies that fit your playing acumen, or are closest to what you'd like to use, appear.

2.   Find a partner who has the same passion for the game as you do—an analytical person who likes to explore possible outcomes and strategies. It's so critical to have another person as jazzed about playing the game as you are, because it makes your training commitment more fun, and provides another perspective or viewpoint to the results you'll both encounter.

3.   Purchase at least *seventeen* decks of cards: one for single deck, two for double deck, six for a six-deck shoe game, and finally eight for an eight-deck shoe game. Additionally, I

seriously recommend visiting a casino supply house and purchasing a shoe, a card discard tray, a layout, and tournament chips to assist in the card dealing and practicing process. Now, this may seem a little over the top, but trust me when I say that having ready-to-go deck configurations saves you a lot of time assembling what you need for a particular configuration. It's a real nightmare if all of a sudden you realize you're missing a king, an ace, or other card; having every configuration at the ready prevents confusion, and you can play at will. If you don't want to make these kinds of purchases, you can scour the Internet for free downloadable software that will assist in training and testing your skills. This option can be very challenging, and it doesn't require a partner for those of you who are unable to find someone who likes this type of pastime as much as you do. Some Web sites that offer tutorials to assist you in gaining more experience playing are *www.bjcenter.com*, *www.bj.com*, *www.borisbj21.com*, and *www.tournamentblackjack.com*.

4. Practice dealing and drawing cards using the playing strategies outlined in this book. Memorize the strategies. Have your partner test you, and you test your partner until you both have the strategies down cold. You should both score at least 98% correct all the time. If you are somewhat familiar with playing blackjack, then two to four weeks of training should do it.

5. Practice and perfect the methods for keeping track of the CLB totals. Remember to assemble two stacks of chips to keep the running total—one stack representing units of five, and the other units of one, as an example. You can, of course, make those stack values commensurate with the units you are betting. Make sure you reset those stacks to zero any time you win in a CLB series!

6. *Optional.* Learn to casual count, because it will assist in giving you valuable information on whether or not to double or split in doubling or splitting situations. Casual counting is used to make card-drawing decisions rather than setting your bet; the betting strategy pretty much takes care of that.

7. Before venturing into the grand territory of casino land where you'll play for real money, play some tournaments first. Tournaments are great proving grounds for testing and honing your skills for very little money, while giving you the on-site exposure to playing actual games with competitors at the tables. It's a great initiation, and you'll be glad you did it! If you can't find any tournaments in your area, throw some blackjack parties at home with a few friends. After all, you already have the cards, the shoe, and the chips; it makes for a really fun evening, and you'll gain great knowledge and possibly get some additional friends interested in going out and joining you to play for real money.

8. Now that you are ready to play for real money, it's time to do a little research and find the establishment that has the deck configuration you like playing and the rules that optimize your chances of winning. Try to find at least two or three establishments that fit the criteria you've set, just to help break up the atmosphere a little.

9. Remember that the hours between 1:00 and 3:00 A.M. are the best time to begin gaming. There are fewer folks around to upset your chances for a win and a lot fewer table jumpers coming in and out of your game.

10. Before walking in to a casino, make sure you have set your intended win and loss limit and stick with it. Make the conscious effort—no exceptions! Ensure that you have the specified bankroll and associated session packets to achieve your win goal.

11. At the casino, carefully look around for a table that suits you according to the deck configuration, number of players, attitude of the dealer, and so on. Take your time and don't be in a hurry to get your money down. Be selective, calm, cool, and carry a *no fear* attitude; think positively because you have a right to. If you've taken the time to get this far, my friends, you are definitely ready to win!

12. Remember to observe casino etiquette. If you want to join a table where there is only one person playing and this

individual is winning, it's always polite to ask if he or she minds if you sit down. If the player invites you to sit, then wait until the shuffle before jumping in. If the player doesn't invite you to sit, you're better off finding another table because this person definitely will not be good to play with. The player may hold a grudge if you do sit down and possibly upset his or her game, so the player might try to destroy some winning opportunities for you by taking cards you may have a chance to draw just to blow you out of the game.

13. No drinking while gaming. This is imperative! You'll need all your wits about you. Don't think for a minute that those casinos offer free drinks because they feel like being benevolent. They're trying to dilute your abilities as quickly as they can. Gambling is a serious business and to win you have to be serious. To be serious, you have to be focused. To be focused, you can't be drunk. Enough said.

14. Never gamble when you're mentally fatigued, tired from no sleep, or emotionally upset. All three are, of course, a recipe for disaster. If mentally fatigued, you'll have no focus. If physically tired, you'll have no patience. If emotionally upset, you may as well strap your judgment to a bottle rocket and watch it soar out of sight.

If you get the butterflies when walking in for your first serious visit to make money, it's okay; we all do, even some of the pros. Getting a little nervous means that you're in touch with the reality of gaming and that you have to be on your toes! As I've said numerous times already, it's time now for *patience* and *discipline*. You've already taken care of everything else. You now need to be congratulated—the challenge awaits you. If you've performed everything on this checklist, you've now become one of the 1% of the gaming population who actually has prepared him- or herself for playing one of the best games in the gaming industry, blackjack. It's the one game that you can actually consistently win at, and you're about to prove that point to yourself!

CASINO COMPS—
MAKING YOUR PLAY, PAY!

You've been putting time in at your favorite casino, and you've probably accrued all kinds of niceties and didn't even realize it. These niceties are the bonus awaiting players of all kinds of games, a veritable treasure for those who know how to earn it, leverage it, and cash in on it! I am often asked, "How much do I have to play in this casino before those guys are going to *comp* me anything?" It's a good question to be sure but deserves a detailed answer. First, for those of you who don't know what a casino comp is, I'll take a moment to explain it. "Comp" is derived from the word "complimentary," and a casino comp is a gift a casino gives to its patrons as a thank-you for playing there. Comps can come in the form of food, hotel rooms, entertainment, apparel, merchandise, airline tickets, limousine service, you name it!

What Determines the Comp?

Whether you play slots, blackjack, roulette, craps, poker, or anything else that you can place a bet on, a casino determines what it will comp you based on (1) what type of game you're playing, (2) how long you've been playing, and (3) how much money you've been consistently betting. All the games in the casino earn comp points at a different rate, so if your intent is to rack up a lot of comp points quickly, you need to play the game that earns you the most points the quickest. Casinos all develop a factor called the EP rating, which stands for *earning power*. Casinos are not so interested in whether you win or lose (of course, they love it when you do lose); they're more concerned with how devastating a player you might be, how much money you put into action per hour, and how much earning power or earning potential you really have—all of which ultimately assists them in calculating how many comp points they intend to award you!

If you wish to earn comp points, and everybody does, then all you need to do is tell the dealer you want your play tracked. The dealer will summon a floor supervisor who will ask you for your player card. If you don't have one, the floor supervisor will be happy to sign you up. As you are playing, the floor supervisor will track your play every ten to fifteen minutes on a tracking that is conveniently tucked behind the table where you are playing, usually to the right of the dealer. The floor supervisor will write down on your card how much he sees you betting at that particular moment. Your information is placed into the casino's player tracking system right there in the pit area, generally by a data entry person, every thirty minutes or so in order to keep the information as current as possible for the casino hosts, the folks who actually award you the comps. Most casinos offer a kiosk that allows players to view how many points they've accumulated so players know when they've reached certain tier levels to receive certain awards. When you use some of your points, they are deducted from your balance. These points generally do not expire.

I highly recommend that if you visit a casino, or even a group of casinos on a regular basis, you become a member of the casino's players club. At the very least, if you're a minimum bettor, you'll be treated to a full meal, or at least a sandwich, every time you visit, and that's worth something, isn't it? I rarely pay for my meals and hotel rooms, which is clear evidence that if I give the casino where I'm staying at least 60% of my action, then I stand a better-than-average chance that the casino will pick up my accommodations, but more on that later in this chapter.

Twelve Games and Their Comp Ratings

Following are some of the more popular casino games, ranked from the highest comp rating (3), to the lowest comp rating (1). The games with the highest ranking earn you the most points in the shortest amount of time. I include the approximate house edge on the game if I have the information.

Roulette (3)

Roulette is the game that earns you're the highest comp points because folks play numerous bets on the layout, which generally add up to quite a bit. The American roulette wheel that contains the zero and double zero has the highest percentage edge against the player (–5.26%). The traditional blackjack player who plays $5 units usually bets much more on roulette—anywhere from $10 to $25 per spin. The allure and the possibilities of high payouts makes everyone do it. Roulette is a real gas to play; so if it's your cup of tea, you'll rack up comp points really quickly.

Slot Machines (3)

Most folks don't know this, but slot machines actually provide casinos with almost 70% of their revenues. Imagine that—70%! I guess that's why we see nothing but slot machines when entering any casino, right? Slot machines actually have a percentage edge against the player of anywhere between –5% to –15%, but most are 15% machines.

And there's only one person who knows where those –5% machines are and that's the manager of the slot machines, who's not telling anyone anything!

Slots are extremely popular with many folks because it requires zero knowledge to play them. All you have to know is how to drop the coins into them and pull the handle or push the spin button! There are no feelings of being judged by others that you aren't playing the game right, there aren't any rules or strategies to memorize, and with a bonus of free drinks while you're playing, what could be simpler?

The average slot player drops anywhere between $100 to $300 in coins into these one-armed bandits during a trip to Las Vegas or any of the other gaming meccas. Granted, in slots the calculation principles are very similar, but it's the overall handle pull or money dropped into the machine that helps the casino assign your points, and not so much the time played at it! There are many variations of slot machines—the style of games, reels versus video, and so on—but one thing is certain: They're all designed to suck the cash right out of your wallet. Every casino has a slot club, so make sure you sign up to get those comp points if you insist on playing these machines.

Caribbean Stud Poker (3)

Here's a game that has gained serious popularity in the last five to six years. Poker players love it. The edge on this game is around –5% against the players. This game is offered in most casinos in the United States, the Bahamas, and of course the Caribbean-based resorts as well.

Let It Ride (2)

This game is another poker derivative that continues to be a favorite among casino patrons and can be found at most casinos in the United States. The approximate edge against the players is around –3.5%.

Three-Card Poker (2)

Here's another popular poker game that's gaining great strides as one of the newest poker offerings. The edge against the players on this one is around –3.5%.

Casino War (2)

Casino war is another game designed for simplicity— whoever has the highest card wins; if you tie, then you go to war with the dealer. The edge against the players on this one is around –2.9%. There are different variations of this game, but the one you want to play is the one that lets you war on all ties with the dealer.

Pai Gow Poker (1)

Pai Gow poker is another poker derivative. It appeals to many folks because it takes a long time to lose your money. You have to beat the dealer's high and low hand to be a winner; there's generally a lot of pushing or tie hands with the dealer in this game. It's played with a combination of dice and cards. The house edge against the player is around –1.5%.

Craps (1)

Craps is the dice thrower's favorite game, and is generally considered one of the best bets in the casino, especially on the come-out roll. The edge against the player on this one is around –1.41%. I would strenuously suggest staying away from the proposition bets on this one because the house's edge goes through the roof on those.

Baccarat (1)

This game is typically a high-stakes one, usually found in most casinos' *salon* or *high-roller* pit areas. It's widely thought to be a reasonably even game between the player and bank hands, however, the edge does go to the bank's hand, vis-à-vis the *third card rule*. The hand that is the closest to nine wins with a maximum of three cards to be dealt to either hand. The house edge against the players versus bank hands on this game oscillates around –1.15% on average.

Spanish 21 (1)

Certainly my favorite game to play! Depending on some rule variations and whether the game is dealt from six or eight decks and whether the dealer stands or hits on soft seventeen, this game is a favorite among 21 players all over the world and can be found in most casinos throughout the United States. The edge against the players can range from –.45% to –.80% on the base part of the game. The edge against the players on the match play for unsuited matches is around –3%.

Video Poker (1)

Believe it or not, this slot machine–type game gives the players an opportunity to utilize some strategy against the electronic world. Video poker has become a favorite for both slot and poker players alike. The house edge against the players on this one is around –.5%.

Blackjack (1)

And finally, here's the game this book is written about, so I needn't explain the game, because you already know all the variations and their associated rules. The house's edge on this game can range from –.2% to around –1% against the player. This game certainly is one of the best games to play in the casino where players can leverage their skill and luck to temporarily overcome the house's edge.

Getting Comp Points *and* Winning

Now that you understand the rankings, how do you gain comp points on the lower-ranked games; that is, the games you have the best chance of winning? Simply put, you have to bet bigger amounts with a higher degree of frequency and consistency. Typically a $5 bettor at the blackjack table playing head-to-head against the dealer wagers at a rate of approximately 100 hands per hour, yielding a total amount wagered of $500, right? That's easy math for you to figure. Okay, so here comes a player who bets *$50* a hand instead of $5. He or she wagers about $5,000 per hour, correct? Same game, different betting, with a bigger chance for either the house to get the player's cash, or the player to demolish the house. At any rate, this player puts more money into action on the table and, therefore, will get greater consideration from the house when it comes to awarding comp points. The house wants this type of player to stay and play, so it offers as many amenities as it can justify to keep the player in its establishment.

So how much does it take to get your accommodations and travel paid for? Casinos in the gaming meccas have tightened up their policies these days, so it's no longer really easy to get comped for rooms and plane tickets. They now expect players to bet, at a minimum, an average bet of anywhere between $75 and $150, three to four hours a day, for three to four days just to get these comps. That equates to wagering $10,000 per hour on average.

Comps Going to the Extreme: High Rollers

Betting $10,000 an hour may seem extreme, but it's quite minor to some of the high rollers who come to places like Las Vegas or any of the other gambling meccas. A high roller is a gambler who maintains a line of credit with a casino of anywhere between $100,000 and $500,000 and is willing to gamble any portion or even all of it during any one visit. Special casino hosts or marketing representatives often invite these players, and they are comped to the max! Generally casinos provide air transportation, hotel, entertainment, golf, massage—you name it, and they'll comp it! High rollers usually bet anywhere between $500 to $5,000 a hand, which makes it easy to understand why casinos roll out the red carpet for these folks. I sat at a table with one of these high rollers at a resort in Lake Tahoe, where he was betting five playing positions at the blackjack table. His bets ranged from $5,000 to $10,000 per hand, which is a lot of cash trading hands at the rate of seventy-five hands per hour. The dealing rate is greatly reduced when high rollers are playing because they like to take their time making their card drawing positions. You can understand why, can't you?

Comps Going to the Extreme: Whales

A whale is a mega player, someone willing to risk anywhere from $1 million to $30 million in any one visit. There are only about 150 to 200 players in the world who fit in this category. They generally gamble anywhere between five and ten times a year and bet anywhere between $25,000 to $150,000 per playing position, sometimes playing three to six positions at the tables. These are serious players!

Of course, the casino really opens the doors to these players! Mega players usually have their own private jets, so the casino pays for their fuel, pilots, plane attendants, landing fees—you get the picture. The casino usually develops what is known as a protocol sheet on every one of these players. This sheet describes in detail how these players like to be treated—how big a suite or bungalow they require and with how many rooms, what kind of champagne or wine they like to drink, how many personal butlers or attendants they require, their favorite food, how many people in their entourage, their likes and dislikes, what nightclubs or restaurants need to be alerted for the player's possible visitation, how many limousines will be required, and the list goes on. Each casino has its own criteria for how mega players earn comps and what the comps are, but this list is definitely in the ballpark for most casinos. Mega players are literally treated as kings and queens from the moment they touch down at the airports. The sky is the limit. These folks take the word *comp* to a whole new level.

THE DIFFERENCE BETWEEN
RECREATIONAL PLAY AND
PROFESSIONAL PLAY

learly, learning how to play blackjack effectively can make a person eager to play all the time. The temptation to play for fun shouldn't be any stronger than the desire to bowl weekly in a league. Many people believe that spending a couple of hours a week at the tables is a relaxation activity like golfing, tennis, skiing, or any other leisure activity. The difference is that gambling, when done correctly, actually nets you money instead of costing you money on the sports and other hobbies you enjoy. In many cases, because of their high initial costs and low resale values, it's more costly to purchase a boat or even Jet Skis, than it is to maintain a love for the game of 21.

The idea here is to perfect your playing and betting strategies so that you actually consistently make money instead of spending it and depreciating it. I actually have friends who consistently win and use their winnings for Christmas presents, vacations, college tuitions, retirement, you name it. It's really nice to see folks perfect a skill, exude the ultimate in discipline, and reap rewards for their well-deserved efforts.

It is important, however, to keep your urge to play in check. For the recreational player, once or twice a week, or possibly four times a month, is reasonable. Keep it simple, short, and profitable. Keep your session victories small and get lots of them, and they will help tremendously in your overall winning attitude and confidence level walking into any casino. It's great to find a buddy to play with. Make it a scheduled thing to do, similar to having a poker night, girls' night out, or something like that. The main idea is to keep it fun and healthful. Having a buddy keeps your playing recreational—each of you helps the other keep your regular games fun, balanced, in check, and always profitable.

Playing professionally or even semiprofessionally takes on a whole different complexion and requires a very serious commitment. Professionals know themselves to the fullest, and they've developed nerves of steel to keep their emotions in check at all times. They always know the odds, always know when profits have been maximized, and always know when to stop. They certainly know the meaning of "tomorrow is another day!" They always know how to find places to play where they can optimize their odds of winning, and they don't usually gamble with others in a night-out scenario. They don't drink while gambling or do anything that keeps their focus off the game.

Professionals treat gambling as if it were a job, and they usually work only three to four days a week. On work days, they usually have a daily regimen just like everyone else: they get up at a specified time, shower, relax, eat a leisurely meal, get dressed (usually with style and class), and then play for about three to four sessions in about four to five hours, usually in the early-morning hours (1:00 to 3:00 A.M.). They usually play anywhere from $25 to $200 units and set profit goals of anywhere between $1,000 and $5,000 daily, sometimes more (usually eighteen to twenty-four units). They always ensure that they have a big enough bankroll in front of them (on the table, not in their pockets!) to endure the battle—at least $10,000 to $15,000 in ready reserve. Professionals must have that kind of cash before they can even think about making a living at gambling.

Professionals show no remorse if they lose, and a tempered satisfaction when they win. To them it's just another day at work. They keep great records of their play for accounting purposes. They track where they gambled, how long they played at each table, how easy or difficult it was to make their goals, notes on casino policies, how they were treated, hotel fees, meals, taxis, car rentals, everything. Additionally, they make notes on their own behavior and how they felt when certain situations arose to create a psychological profile of themselves that they can critique and learn from. Professionals reflect on their own behavior, look for recurring patterns that end up being nonproductive, and make changes if necessary.

Professional gamblers with serious commitments to understanding themselves, the odds, the games, and the variations can generally make anywhere from $100,000 to $500,000 per year working less than half the time the rest of us do at our nine-to-five jobs, but there is a price. The tension and the emotional roller coaster is ten times greater and can make a person age quickly. Many pros make a point of taking up golf, swimming, getting frequent massages, you name it, just to take the edge off the stress of their careers. Many folks believe that a professional's life is *glamorous,* but trust me when I say it isn't. After a while all the casinos seem the same, and the deafening sounds of the slot machines, screaming drunks, and out-of-control players become routine, just like any other workplace.

So ask yourself, could this be you someday? Who knows? The information in this book will help get you there if that's a place you want to be. But remember, just knowing the mechanics of play is only the half the equation; the other half is called character!

I wish you the best of luck in your gaming endeavors and hope that each one of you becomes a *21 gun!*

USING CLB STRATEGY FOR BACCARAT

T he CLB strategy works with other popular even-money proposition games, as well, notably the game of baccarat. I won't go into the details of how baccarat is played and will assume you know that already. What's interesting is that we, the players, really have no influence over the outcome of each winning hand. It's strictly determined by the rules of play. In baccarat, all we can do as players is decide which hand to bet on, player or banker, and how much to bet. So, how do we mount an offensive posture using the CLB strategy and the mathematical nuances of the game?

Baccarat—The High-Stakes Game

Baccarat is actually one of the best betting games, next to blackjack, in the casino. The odds are pretty even between the player and the banker hand, with a slight edge going to the banker hand because of how third card rules are structured. Out of every 100 hands played or dealt, the banker hand wins an average of 50.62% of the hands, and the player hand wins an average of 49.38%. Tie hands (hands neither the banker nor the player wins or loses) are not counted here. The house's edge on the banker hands is only a fraction less than the percentage on the player hands.

The win statistics are important because they assist you in deciding when to place a bet and on which hand. Baccarat and roulette are similar in that you can observe while being seated at the table with chips in front of you, and not be required to bet every round. I'm a devotee of baccarat, more-so than roulette, because I'm a "law of equal distribution" or "law of large numbers" kind of guy. If I had my druthers, I'd always pick baccarat over roulette because I've got a fixed sample of cards to draw from, compared to infinite sequences of spins on the roulette wheel.

If the banker hand has the edge, why don't you just bet banker all the time? That's not a bad strategy, and there are pros and statisticians out there who do just that. However, to do that you have to pay the house a 5% commission on every winning banker hand and that can get expensive, because you're not getting a true 1:1 payout. You're getting only a 19:20 payout; therefore, if you win, let's say, an average of $2,000 per shoe betting on the banker hand, you'll pay the house $100 in commissions for the privilege, yielding you a net of only $1,900. Play ten shoes a session, and it gets really expensive! It's for this reason that I prefer playing the player hand more than the banker hand, but I do play both if the percentages are there.

What I do is wait for an opportune moment to start the betting sequence as soon as a certain set of parameters is met. Okay, what parameters? Following are the parameters, or rules, I set prior to committing to a bet sequence. You can create your own parameters, but let's set some right here for the purposes of analysis.

Condition 1: Set the Profit and Loss Goal

Nothing new here—you did this for blackjack, Spanish 21, and any derivative—so you do the same for this game as well.

In baccarat, where the stakes can get extremely high very quickly, you must set your limits and adhere to them religiously. I like to set a six- to eight-unit goal per shoe, which may seem like a low profit goal, but remember, baccarat is a high-stakes game and the table minimums are usually *$25* to *$100*.

Condition 2: Set the Initial Wait Period

I believe it's prudent to wait an *absolute minimum* of five hands and preferably up to ten hands to see if the percentages bear out or to possibly spot a trend surfacing. Don't be in a hurry to get a bet down. Wait and be patient—patience is *golden* at these games!

Condition 3: Set the Percentage for the Player Bet Commitment

The banker hand, not counting tics, should win approximately 51% of the time, on average. Therefore, I'll set the percentage win ratio for banker outcomes at a minimum of 56% to 58% before I place a bet for the *player* hand. The extra 5% allows for win streaks by the banker hand for as many as six to eight consecutive hands, which happens many times more for the banker hand than it does for the player hand. It's important to note that you'll see large swings in the percentages in the beginning of the shoe, usually hands one through twenty, and then the percentages start to converge. That's why it's prudent to set yourself some tier levels of percentage values as the shoe progresses to different stages.

Condition 4: Set the Percentage for the Banker Bet Commitment

You need to decide when to begin playing the banker hand. If you see the percentage of the banker hand drop below 48%, especially midway through the shoe, start your betting sequence at this point. If you are tenths of point away from making a decision, take your best shot; remember, intuition does play an important part in playing this game—just try your best to stay within the guidelines you set for yourself. You may wish to adjust percentage levels here as the hands are being dealt and the true odds of player and banker surface and begin to converge.

Condition 5: Set the Consecutive Win Limit

Remember, this is a 51:49 game, excluding the tie hands, so winning three in a row really is a pretty good streak. Even if parameters dictate that you should make a bet, stop—don't do it—wait for the next series of bet changes, or you may get caught in a losing streak and really take a beating. I seriously don't recommend placing another bet. But if you really want to go farther, make sure you bet only the table minimum. That way, if you lose, you won't destroy your previous win profits.

Condition 6: Once a Bet Sequence Is Initiated, Stick with It!

Once you begin a bet sequence see it through even if the betting parameters fall above or below the initial parameters that initiated the sequence.

Condition 7: Set the Hand at Which You'll Stop Before Making Another Bet Sequence!

As you progress toward the end of the shoe you need to decide beforehand on which hand you'll stop initiating and analyzing for a bet sequence. Since there are usually only seventy-three to eighty hands, on average, dealt in a baccarat shoe, you certainly don't want to begin a bet sequence and have the shoe end on you. Let's say you just finished a winning sequence at hand 63 and the bet parameters indicate that you need to make a bet five hands later. If you've set your stop-bet parameter at hand 70, you should forgo making any further bets because the shoe could finish up just when you're making a CLB bet, ruining your opportunity to recover your losses for the sequence.

Okay, now that I've set the conditions to initiate the betting sequences, I want to show you how to keep track of the percentages, what tools to use, and what kind of scorecard you need to keep track of all this. Let's first look at the scorecard that appears in Figure A-1; it's specially designed to capture the information you need to make your betting decisions. You can copy this scorecard, or fashion your own with a form-making or spreadsheet program.

- **Bet action**: Here you note what action you plan for the next outcome of cards. You would note either:
  Wait—Stand by to assess the next outcome without making a bet.
  Bank—Place a bet on the next hand for the banker.
  Plyr—Place a bet on the next hand for the player.
- **Amt bet**: Note here the amount to be wagered on the next hand. Indicate "none" if a wait mode has occurred.
- **Bank**: Indicate here with a mark if the outcome is a banker hand.
- **No.**: Indicate here the ascending quantity of banker hands, of course incremented by one each time a banker hand occurs.
- **Plyer**: Indicate here with a mark if the outcome is a player hand.
- **No.**: Indicate here the ascending quantity of player hands, of course incremented by one each time a player hand occurs.
- **Hands dealt**: Note in ascending order and incrementally the number for each banker and player outcome only, not the tie hands. From this you can assess the percentage of banker hands versus player hands. *Do* note that the tie hand occurred; just don't count it in assessing the percentage.
- **Tie**: Indicate here with a mark if the outcome is a tie hand.

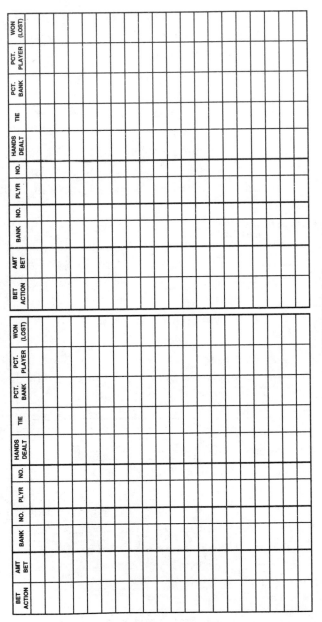

FIGURE A-1

- **Pct. bank:** This is the percentage of banker hands versus banker/player hands dealt, not including tie hands.
- **Pct. player:** This is the percentage of player hands versus banker/player hands dealt, not including tie hands.
- **Won (Lost):** Note whether the wager you placed wins or loses.

After setting the parameters for when to start betting, now you have to set the betting parameters. As I indicated earlier, in the beginning of a shoe you usually see wide swings in percentages of outcomes. It's best to wait, in my opinion, at least ten hands to see how things begin to flush out. But as the shoe progresses you'll see the percentages of player versus banker outcomes converge. As each ten or so hands pass, you will see a definite change, so you need to set parameters for betting as each ten hands passes. Following is a chart (Figure A-2) I'll use as an example of how to set these parameters. Please note that these parameters are the ones I use, and you may change them according to your own preferences.

	IS ABOVE	START HAND	END HAND
BET PLAYER IF "BANK":	65.0%	11	20
BET BANK IF "PLAYER":	58.0%	11	20
BET PLAYER IF "BANK":	60.0%	21	30
BET BANK IF "PLAYER":	56.0%	21	30
BET PLAYER IF "BANK":	58.0%	31	40
BET BANK IF "PLAYER":	54.0%	31	40
BET PLAYER IF "BANK":	55.5%	41	50
BET BANK IF "PLAYER":	53.0%	41	50
BET PLAYER IF "BANK":	54.8%	51	60
BET BANK IF "PLAYER":	52.0%	51	60
BET PLAYER IF "BANK":	53.5%	61	70
BET BANK IF "PLAYER":	51.5%	61	70

FIGURE A-2

Looking at Figure A-2, you see on hands 11 through 20 you would place a bet on the player hand if the banker hand is equal to or greater than 65%, or if the same player hand is equal to or less than 35%. And as you can see, these percentage parameters are broken down for each ten hands as you step through the shoe. Typically you'll see these percentages begin to converge as the hands are being dealt and you progress through the shoe. By setting betting parameters and parameters for when to start betting, you help protect yourself from being on the wrong betting side when long losing streaks occur.

Figure A-3 shows an example of what a scorecard should look like once you begin filling it in. Please note how I skipped numbering the tie hand outcomes. This scorecard shows thirty-eight hands and represents how you might start from the beginning of the shoe. Remember, you are analyzing, in this case, the results from hand 9 before making a wait, banker, or player decision on hand 10, and so on.

As you can see in Figure A-3, after you make only eleven bets, you're already almost 4.5 units ahead with minimum exposure on compounding bets. Through this illustration you can see that making the six- to eight-unit goal is generally quite achievable.

It might seem awkward to use a calculator to figure out percentages right at the table, however, this is the best method to keep an accurate analysis and you're allowed to do it. Therefore, I highly recommend doing so unless you're a math wizard and can do them in your head. The full game of baccarat (at the large formal tables) is usually played with eight decks of cards, although in some casinos it's played with six decks. Some casinos offer mini-baccarat, which is played the same as full baccarat, but on a blackjack-sized table. I believe it's important to note that mini-bach, as it's called, is dealt much faster than baccarat played at the large format tables, because the dealer turns over the cards for both the banker and the player hands. At the large tables the players

	BET ACTION	AMT BET	BANK	NO.	PLYR	NO.	HANDS DEALT	TIE	PCT. BANK	PCT. PLYR	WON (LOST)
1	WAIT	NA	/	1			1		100.0%	0.0%	NA
2	WAIT	NA	/	2			2		100.0%	0.0%	NA
3	WAIT	NA	/	3			3		100.0%	0.0%	NA
4	WAIT	NA			/	1	4		75.0%	25.0%	NA
5	WAIT	NA	/	4			5		80.0%	20.0%	NA
6	WAIT	NA			/	2	6		66.6%	33.4%	NA
7	WAIT	NA			/	3	7		57.1%	42.9%	NA
8	WAIT	NA	/	5			8		62.5%	37.5%	NA
9	WAIT	NA	/	6			9		66.6%	33.4%	NA
10	WAIT	NA			/	4	10		60.0%	40.0%	NA
11	PLYR	$25						/	60.0%	40.0%	NA
12	PLYR	$25			/	5	11		54.5%	45.5%	WON
13	WAIT	NA	/	7			12		58.3%	41.7%	NA
14	WAIT	NA	/	8			13		61.5%	38.5%	NA
15	PLYR	$25			/	6	14		57.1%	42.9%	WON
16	WAIT	NA			/	7	15		53.3%	46.7%	NA
17	WAIT	NA			/	8	16		50.0%	50.0%	NA
18	WAIT	NA	/	9			17		52.9%	47.1%	NA
19	WAIT	NA	/	10			18		55.5%	44.5%	NA
20	WAIT	NA			/	9	19		52.6%	47.4%	NA
21	WAIT	NA			/	10	20		50.0%	50.0%	NA
22	WAIT	NA			/	11	21		47.6%	52.4%	NA
23	WAIT	NA			/	12	22		45.4%	54.6%	NA
24	BANK	$25			/	13	23		43.4%	56.6%	LOST
25	BANK	$35	/	11			24		45.8%	54.2%	WON
26	BANK	$25						/	45.8%	54.2%	LOST
27	BANK	$35	/	12			25		48.0%	52.0%	WON
28	WAIT	NA						/	48.0%	52.0%	NA
29	WAIT	NA			/	14	26		46.1%	53.9%	NA
30	BANK	$25			/	15	27		44.4%	55.6%	LOST
31	BANK	$35	/	13			28		46.4%	53.6%	WON
32	BANK	$25	/	14			29		48.2%	51.8%	WON
33	WAIT	NA	/	15			30		50.0%	50.0%	NA
34	WAIT	NA	/	16			31		51.6%	48.4%	NA
35	WAIT	NA	/	17			32		53.1%	46.9%	NA
36	WAIT	NA	/	18			33		54.5%	45.5%	NA
37	PLYR	$25	/	19			34		55.8%	44.2%	LOST
38	PLYR	$35			/	16	35		54.3%	45.7%	WON

FIGURE A-3

themselves are passed the shoe and allowed to deal and turn over the cards. The game slows down at large tables because many players make a ritual of taking their time inspecting and subsequently turning over the cards. It's almost monotonous to wait for these players to go through their gyrations just to see what the outcome is. Anyway, back to the foundation of eight decks. Let's look at what we can expect:

Cards per deck 52
Decks used for play 8
Total cards in the shoe 416
Average cards used per deal 5
Cards left behind the cut card 14
Cards actually available for play 402
Estimated number of deals per shoe 80
Estimated percentage of tie hands
   per shoe 9.5%
Estimated number of tie hands 8
After *ties,* hands left distributed
   between banker and player 72
Estimated percentage of banker
   hands per shoe 51%
Estimated number of banker hands
   to be seen 37
Estimated number of player hands
   to be seen 35

Now you can see what the realities of the game really are. It usually takes about seventy-five to ninety minutes to go through an entire eight-deck shoe at a medium pace, assuming you don't have too many ritualistic card turners at the table. But it's just not the card turners who take all the time. It's also the folks who take forever to decide what hand to bet on. The dealers won't deal the game until all the bets have been decided and placed, and waiting for these slowpokes to make up their minds can be very agitating, believe me; on average it takes about forty-five to sixty seconds for everyone to make those decisions between dealt hands at a fully occupied baccarat table, in some cases longer.

Okay, now that we understand how to fill in the tracking card, we now need to make a determination on when to place a bet. To get a better look at what type of shoe you might encounter, I encourage and highly recommend that you wait and track a minimum of ten to fifteen hands before making any bets at all. Tracking hands is crucial because most times, you'll get very valuable information on what type of shoe you'll be heading into—a player-favored shoe, a banker-favored shoe, or a choppy shoe (a shoe that alternates back and forth between player and banker every one to two hands). This information is beneficial in the following way. If you are experiencing a *player*-favored shoe with most of them coming consecutively, then, of course, you would most likely be betting on the *banker* hand. However, once you've won a betting sequence on the banker hand, sometimes it's better to wait for a few more player hands to go by before reinitiating a bet on the banker hand again even though the percentages indicate that you should. Using this type of scrutiny will prevent you from having to make every bet on the banker just because the percentages are in line and the percentage breakdowns in Figure A-2 tell you to do so. Sometimes during an entire shoe, as in this example I just explained, the banker hand percentages will never catch up with the player hand percentages. Again, the idea for using this percentage methodology is to keep the amount of wagers to a minimum and look for small windows of opportunities to capitalize on and win.

You've waited the recommended number of hands and you now have to make the calculations. Simply add the sum total of player and banker hands; then determine the calculation for the player by dividing the total hands into the amount of player hands. You'll derive the ratio percentage; do the same for the banker hand. There are instances when neither betting percentage condition is met wherein you just go into *wait* mode.

Clearly, there will come a time when you will experience a player shoe where the player hands exceed all expectations and demolish the banker hands by a score of forty-eight player hands versus thirty-two banker hands, or vice versa. It doesn't happen often enough, but it does happen with some degree of regularity. What I find exceptionally interesting is that most serious baccarat players don't understand the potentially huge rewards they could get just by keeping track of these percentages and statistics. Instead they'll bet the farm on a banker hand after ten straight wins. It makes no sense to me. Sure, you could make the bet and ride the streak, but if your chart says the banker hand at this point is at 65% or greater and you've already seen sixty-six player/banker hands dealt, I'd sure want to see the shoe even out a bit with some player hands coming soon.

There are no guarantees; baccarat is almost a 50:50 game, and most players bet their intuition and not the percentages. The best way to see if the CLB strategy works for you coupled with this percentage method is to visit a casino, sit close to an active baccarat table, and begin tracking for yourself. I believe you'll be astonished at how effective the coupled strategies can be in most cases and you will get some pretty interesting and pleasing results. Now let's take you through the CLB strategy and see what happens.

The stage is set, and you have your betting strategy lined out. This, of course, is totally changeable according to your playing acumen and bankroll situation. To play the semiconservative strategy shown in Figure A-4, I recommend a bankroll of at least $1,250, with a $1,250 backup. Baccarat is, in my opinion, not as volatile as blackjack, so you don't need a third-session packet, especially since you're going for merely a six- to eight-unit goal per shoe played. Because the stakes and subsequent bet units are higher in baccarat, it's easier to leave after two or three shoes. Figure A-6 shows a run of one shoe so you can see how the betting and percentage parameters work in concert with one another.

BACCARAT CLB STRATEGY - MODEL 7
Semi-Conservative CLB-ZONE Stage Betting
(For a $25 Minimum Table and/or Base Unit size)

Baccarat Betting LOSS Schema

Bet Code	Bet Amount	WHEN WIN GO TO	IF LOSS GO TO
THE ZONE			
L1	$25	W1	L2
L2	$35	W1	L3
L3	$65	W1	L4
L4	$140	W1	L5
L5	80-CLB	W1	L6
CLB STAGE 2			
L6	$25	W6	L6
L7	90-CLB	W1	L8
L8	$25	W6	L8

Baccarat Betting WIN Schema

Bet Code	Bet Amount	IF WIN GO TO	IF LOSS GO TO
THE ZONE			
W1	$25	W2	L2
W2	$35	W3	L2
W3	$25	W4	L2
W4	$35	W5	L2
W5	$25	W4	L2
CLB STAGE 2			
W6	80-CLB	W1	L7

FIGURE A-4

FIGURE A-5

BACCARAT RUN FOR (80) RESULTS - $25 BET UNITS - MODEL 7

HAND NO.	BET TYPE	BET CODE	BET AMT	RESULT	HAND WON	PCT. BNKR	PCT. PLYR	GAIN (LOSS)	RUNNING BALANCE	CLB ACCRUAL
1	WAIT	NONE	$0	NA	BANK	100.0%	0.0%	$0	$0	$0
2	WAIT	NONE	$0	NA	PLYR	50.0%	50.0%	$0	$0	$0
3	WAIT	NONE	$0	NA	PLYR	33.3%	66.7%	$0	$0	$0
4	WAIT	NONE	$0	NA	BANK	50.0%	50.0%	$0	$0	$0
5	WAIT	NONE	$0	NA	BANK	60.0%	40.0%	$0	$0	$0
6	WAIT	NONE	$0	NA	BANK	66.7%	33.3%	$0	$0	$0
7	WAIT	NONE	$0	NA	PLYR	57.1%	42.9%	$0	$0	$0
8	WAIT	NONE	$0	NA	BANK	62.5%	37.5%	$0	$0	$0
9	WAIT	NONE	$0	NA	PLYR	55.6%	44.4%	$0	$0	$0
10	WAIT	NONE	$0	NA	BANK	60.0%	40.0%	$0	$0	$0
11	WAIT	NONE	$0	NA	BANK	63.6%	36.4%	$0	$0	$0
12	WAIT	NONE	$0	NA	PLYR	58.3%	41.7%	$0	$0	$0
13	WAIT	NONE	$0	NA	PLYR	53.8%	46.2%	$0	$0	$0
14	WAIT	NONE	$0	NA	TIE	53.8%	46.2%	$0	$0	$0
15	WAIT	NONE	$0	NA	BANK	57.1%	42.9%	$0	$0	$0
16	WAIT	NONE	$0	NA	PLYR	53.3%	46.7%	$0	$0	$0
17	WAIT	NONE	$0	NA	BANK	56.3%	43.8%	$0	$0	$0

HAND NO.	BET TYPE	BET CODE	BET AMT	RESULT	HAND WON	PCT. BNKR	PCT. PLYR	GAIN (LOSS)	RUNNING BALANCE	CLB ACCRUAL
18	WAIT	NONE	$0	NA	BANK	58.8%	41.2%	$0	$0	$0
19	WAIT	NONE	$0	NA	BANK	61.1%	38.9%	$0	$0	$0
20	WAIT	NONE	$0	NA	PLYR	57.9%	42.1%	$0	$0	$0
21	WAIT	NONE	$0	NA	BANK	60.0%	40.0%	$0	$0	$0
22	WAIT	NONE	$0	NA	TIE	60.0%	40.0%	$0	$0	$0
23	WAIT	NONE	$0	NA	PLYR	57.1%	42.9%	$0	$0	$0
24	WAIT	NONE	$0	NA	BANK	59.1%	40.9%	$0	$0	$0
25	WAIT	NONE	$0	NA	BANK	60.9%	39.1%	$0	$0	$0
26	PLYR	W1	$25	L	BANK	62.5%	37.5%	($25)	($25)	($25)
27	PLYR	L1	$25	WIN	PLYR	60.0%	40.0%	$25	$0	$0
28	WAIT	NONE	$0	NA	TIE	60.0%	40.0%	$0	$0	$0
29	WAIT	NONE	$0	NA	BANK	61.5%	38.5%	$0	$0	$0
30	PLYR	W1	$25	NA	TIE	61.5%	38.5%	$0	$0	$0
31	PLYR	W1	$25	L	BANK	63.0%	37.0%	($25)	($25)	($25)
32	PLYR	L1	$25	WIN	PLYR	60.7%	39.3%	$25	$0	$0
33	PLYR	W1	$25	WIN	PLYR	58.6%	41.4%	$25	$25	$0
34	PLYR	W2	$35	NA	TIE	58.6%	41.4%	$0	$25	$0
35	PLYR	W2	$35	WIN	PLYR	56.7%	43.3%	$35	$60	$0
36	WAIT	NONE	$0	NA	BANK	58.1%	41.9%	$0	$60	$0

HAND NO.	BET TYPE	BET CODE	BET AMT	RESULT	HAND WON	PCT. BNKR	PCT. PLYR	GAIN (LOSS)	RUNNING BALANCE	CLB ACCRUAL
37	PLYR	W1	$25	L	BANK	59.4%	40.6%	($25)	$35	($25)
38	PLYR	L1	$25	L	BANK	60.6%	39.4%	($25)	$10	($50)
39	PLYR	L2	$35	L	BANK	61.8%	38.2%	($35)	($25)	($85)
40	PLYR	L3	$65	WIN	PLYR	60.0%	40.0%	$65	$40	($20)
41	PLYR	W1	$25	WIN	PLYR	58.3%	41.7%	$25	$65	$0
42	PLYR	W2	$35	WIN	PLYR	56.8%	43.2%	$35	$100	$0
43	PLYR	W3	$25	WIN	PLYR	55.3%	44.7%	$25	$125	$0
44	WAIT	NONE	$0	NA	PLYR	53.8%	46.2%	$0	$125	$0
45	WAIT	NONE	$0	NA	PLYR	52.5%	47.5%	$0	$125	$0
46	WAIT	NONE	$0	NA	PLYR	51.2%	48.8%	$0	$125	$0
47	WAIT	NONE	$0	NA	PLYR	50.0%	50.0%	$0	$125	$0
48	WAIT	NONE	$0	NA	BANK	51.2%	48.8%	$0	$125	$0
49	WAIT	NONE	$0	NA	BANK	52.3%	47.7%	$0	$125	$0
50	WAIT	NONE	$0	NA	BANK	53.3%	46.7%	$0	$125	$0
51	WAIT	NONE	$0	NA	BANK	54.3%	45.7%	$0	$125	$0
52	WAIT	NONE	$0	NA	BANK	55.3%	44.7%	$0	$125	$0
53	PLYR	W1	$25	WIN	PLYR	54.2%	45.8%	$25	$150	$0
54	WAIT	NONE	$0	NA	PLYR	53.1%	46.9%	$0	$150	$0
55	WAIT	NONE	$0	NA	PLYR	52.0%	48.0%	$0	$150	$0

HAND NO.	BET TYPE	BET CODE	BET AMT	RESULT	HAND WON	PCT. BNKR	PCT. PLYR	GAIN (LOSS)	RUNNING BALANCE	CLB ACCRUAL
56	WAIT	NONE	$0	NA	TIE	52.0%	48.0%	$0	$150	$0
57	WAIT	NONE	$0	NA	TIE	52.0%	48.0%	$0	$150	$0
58	WAIT	NONE	$0	NA	BANK	52.9%	47.1%	$0	$150	$0
59	WAIT	NONE	$0	NA	BANK	53.8%	46.2%	$0	$150	$0
60	WAIT	NONE	$0	NA	TIE	53.8%	46.2%	$0	$150	$0
61	PLYR	W1	$25	L	BANK	54.7%	45.3%	($25)	$125	($25)
62	PLYR	L1	$25	WIN	PLYR	53.7%	46.3%	$25	$150	$0
63	PLYR	W1	$25	L	BANK	54.5%	45.5%	($25)	$125	($25)
64	PLYR	L1	$25	L	BANK	55.4%	44.6%	($25)	$100	($50)
65	PLYR	L2	$35	WIN	PLYR	54.4%	45.6%	$35	$135	($15)
66	PLYR	W1	$25	L	BANK	55.2%	44.8%	($25)	$110	($40)
67	PLYR	L1	$25	WIN	PLYR	54.2%	45.8%	$25	$135	($15)
68	PLYR	W1	$25	WIN	PLYR	53.3%	46.7%	$25	$160	$0
69	WAIT	NONE	$0	NA	PLYR	52.5%	47.5%	$0	$160	$0
70	WAIT	NONE	$0	NA	BANK	53.2%	46.8%	$0	$160	$0
71	WAIT	NONE	$0	NA	TIE	53.2%	46.8%	$0	$160	$0
72	WAIT	NONE	$0	NA	TIE	53.2%	46.8%	$0	$160	$0
73	WAIT	NONE	$0	NA	PLYR	52.4%	47.6%	$0	$160	$0
74	WAIT	NONE	$0	NA	PLYR	51.6%	48.4%	$0	$160	$0

HAND NO.	BET TYPE	BET CODE	BET AMT	RESULT	HAND WON	PCT. BNKR	PCT. PLYR	GAIN (LOSS)	RUNNING BALANCE	CLB ACCRUAL
75	WAIT	NONE	$0	NA	BANK	52.3%	47.7%	$0	$160	$0
76	WAIT	NONE	$0	NA	PLYR	51.5%	48.5%	$0	$160	$0
77	WAIT	NONE	$0	NA	PLYR	50.7%	49.3%	$0	$160	$0
78	WAIT	NONE	$0	NA	BANK	51.5%	48.5%	$0	$160	$0
79	WAIT	NONE	$0	NA	PLYR	50.7%	49.3%	$0	$160	$0
80	WAIT	NONE	$0	NA	BANK	51.4%	48.6%	$0	$160	$0

SESSION STATISTICS

	CLB LEVEL 1	110%
	CLB LEVEL 2	90%
	CLB LEVEL 3	80%
	Goal for the session	**$150**
	Estimated hands per hour	40
	Maximum Table Limit	$500

Highest bet made in the entire CLB series	**$65**
What hand did we make that bet?	40
What was the balance at that time?	($25)

Longest losing streak*	**3**
*(TIES continue the streak, but are not counted)	
Dollars wagered in that losing streak	$85

Highest balance achieved	**$160**
At what hand?	68

Lowest balance experienced	**($25)**
At what hand?	26

Goal amount achieved	**$160**
At what hand achieved?	68
Minutes required to achieve goal	102.0
Dollars wagered to reach the goal	$690
# of bets to reach goal	24
Total R.O.I. upon reaching goal	**23.19%**

Ending SHOE balance	**$160**
Total Dollars wagered in the entire SHOE	$690
Total R.O.I. - the entire SHOE	**23.19%**

No. of CLB-L1 bets to reach goal?	**0**
No. of CLB-L2 bets to reach goal?	**0**
No. of CLB-L3 bets to reach goal?	**0**

No. of CLB-L1 Bets in the entire series?	**0**
No. of CLB-L2 Bets in the entire series?	**0**
No. of CLB-L3 Bets in the entire series?	**0**

42.50%	**PLYR**	34
45.00%	**BANK**	36
12.50%	**TIES**	10
100.00%	**TOTAL**	80

FIGURE A-6

Figure A-6 shows statistics for you to analyze the results. The most important thing to remember: Get out once your goal is reached for the shoe! Never try to extend the win. If, by chance, a CLB bet places you two units over your goal and you believe you're on a streak, by all means go for it; but lock up your goal money first and just play with the extra. Dump 50% of your continuing profits into the locked-up money pile, and you'll always come out ahead.

Figure A-6 clearly shows that if you bail out once you achieved your goal you have a much better return on your investment, less aggravation with the "ritualistic card turners," and certainly less stress awaiting results. In addition, when you played the banker hand, you paid your commission as you went along to ensure that all the funds are yours upon completion of the shoe. You didn't have to make any CLB bets, which is always good. Using the strategy in Figure A-4 puts you at risk for losing an average of only two bets, and only three to four at most, because you must wait until the percentages are optimized for a ready return.

My strategy may seem a bit radical to some, but to me, a statistics-minded individual, it's the best way to decide which hand to place a bet on. On initial outings I found myself going crazy trying to make the right decisions—player or banker? banker or player?—but my strategy takes out all the guess-work and lets the numbers make the decisions for me.

A note about the unit goals in baccarat: Six to eight units may seem like an unrealistic gain as each shoe is played, but remember, most baccarat players play $100 to $200 hands, if not more, so you're looking at a potential gain of between $600 to $800 per shoe on the low side, to $1,200 and $1,600 on the high side. Those are decent profits for about ninety minutes of work!

I hope my method, at the very least, makes interesting reading to all the baccarat devotees out there, and I wish you all good fortune!

INDEX